Progressive Conversations

Progressive Conversations

Essays on Matters of Social Justice for Critical Thinkers

Roger L. Ray

Foreword by
Brian J. Atra

RESOURCE *Publications* • Eugene, Oregon

PROGRESSIVE CONVERSATIONS
Essays on Matters of Social Justice for Critical Thinkers

Resource Publications
An Imprint of Wipf and Stock Publishers
199 W. 8th Ave., Suite 3
Eugene, OR 97401

www.wipfandstock.com

PAPERBACK ISBN: 978-1-4982-3470-2
HARDCOVER ISBN: 978-1-4982-3472-6

Manufactured in the U.S.A.

Contents

CONTENTS

Section IV: Religious, Philosophical, and Personal

Foreword

Books, like the people who write them and read them, are unique. Both books and people are, in part, the intriguing result of a combination of factors, including life-setting, viewpoint, and culture, to name just a few. This work has been forged in the daily grind of an activist life, daring to rise above the fray, to see the bigger picture, to ask tough questions, and to point us toward solutions and to action.

These conversations are progressive. Simplistic solutions, pat answers, platitudes, cumbersome traditions, and ancient myths and superstitions yield to the light of reasoned inquiry, a starting point for both sound ethics and practical religion, two streams flowing from this timely book.

Roger Ray came into my life through his writing. The pieces included here were composed over many years as newspaper columns in quintessentially conservative Springfield, Missouri, my home when many of these columns were written. They refreshed my spirit after having seen too many "God, Guns, And Guts" bumper stickers and thousands of "WWJD" bracelets. The former are still plentiful, though the latter mostly disappeared after September 11, 2001. Some local color is preserved, yet Roger Ray's voice speaks to a far wider audience. This book deserves to be read, re-read, and studied.

One might well ask, "If these are conversations, where is the voice of the right?" My reply would be that, contrary to what is often purveyed, most of us have already heard the right, far more often than is warranted by tired clichés. Who among us has not repeatedly heard, "I'd rather fight the war on terrorism in Iraq than fight it at home?" In an earlier era, how many of us heard conniving murderers called "freedom fighters?" This book gives voice to the other side, a contrary but honest viewpoint, sometimes brutally so, but always with evidence.

Reasonable people, religious or otherwise, demand evidence, not just sentiment. They seek to base their lives, including faith and ethics, on evidence. So, this book is relevant and welcome.

As a reader, one might make use of this book in several ways. It's a good read straight through. The sections can be read, or re-read, as one refers to various issues. Hence, Progressive Conversations is an ideal reference resource.

College professors, myself among them, could use selected readings interspersed with the theories presented in any of the standard ethics textbooks. The material makes an ideal supplemental text for a semester.

Study groups will find that the book's organization is quite accessible. The overall length is ideally suited for a weekly session extended over three months, typical of church and Sunday school curricula which are often based upon quarters. Ministers, myself among them, may find here both inspiration and illustration. Open minds may learn; cob-webbed minds may become uncluttered.

Roger Ray writes like a preacher. Progressive Conversations conveys prophetic witness and call to action, but tempers this burdensome task with humor. So, enjoy the book. Laugh, get angry, and maybe even cry a bit. Join the conversation. Then get up and live a renewed, more ethical life!

Brian J. Atra, Ph.D.
The University of Southern Indiana

Preface

There is a reason why people have historically used newspapers to start fires and to line the bottom of birdcages. Once a newspaper is a day or two old, its value becomes negligible. I had a generation-long writing relationship with the NewsLeader in Springfield, Missouri. My column evolved from a monthly religion and ethics feature into a weekly column entitled "From the Left." As the universe of print media went into sharp decline, my weekly musings slowly devolved into shorter and less often appearances until my unvarnished liberal views became too much for an increasingly conservative print media.

Collections of newspaper essays are almost always motivated more by narcissism than by relevance, so I will insist that I have worked on this collection under protest. With more than a thousand published columns to look through, it was easy to dismiss the pieces that were too closely tied to a particular event. Even I am no longer able to muster anger at Rush Limbaugh for calling Sandra Fluke a "slut." Actually, on second thought, I can already hear the pulse in my ears when I remember that event, but I don't expect you to necessarily share in that visceral response and so that column is in the recycle bin waiting to become cat litter.

I have selected the columns that address matters of ethics deserving a second reading, some intelligent conversation, and, hopefully, conviction to do something about it. I have tried to minimize regional references or any time-limited illustrations though, unavoidably, these edited essays are based on newspaper opinion columns written by a particular professor and pastor in a mid-sized Midwestern city's newspaper.

It is my hope that these essays will prompt meaningful conversation in college classrooms and among gatherings of adults in book studies, Sunday classes, or an occasional Socrates Café. I have chosen to put a few discussion questions before each essay rather than at the end. I suspect that many discussion groups will hardly need to know what I think. Most of the groups I have been in needed only a topic and an opportunity and the discussion takes off like a rabbit. But please, don't just get mad. Do something.

Acknowledgments

This collection would never have found its way into print were it not for the urging of friends, church members and readers. I must thank the members of Community Christian Church of Springfield, Missouri for their years of support and encouragement generally and specifically for being willing to spend months of discussion group time considering each of the essays in this book. There are two people whose enthusiasm for bringing this collection into print who were much more than merely helpful. Dr. Brian Atra continually read and organized essays, helping to select the ones to include and trying to put the collection into an edited and useful whole. Brian has been a good friend and a consistently brave soul, prodding me to get the project done and bolstering my belief that old newspaper opinion columns could have a useful second life. My friend, Sarah Linda Jacobs, spent many hours editing each essay with a precision that has made me give up my title of "Captain Grammar." Brian and Sarah worked together to make this a readable, relevant, and useful resource and I will be forever grateful to them both.

SECTION I

Political

1

Government

While conservative pundits call Obama a Socialist and worse, the truth appears to be that he may be just a more articulate version of previous, dishonest rightwing office holders.

An Oligarchy at Best

If donating money is a form of political speech, then aren't we giving the wealthy the ability to vote more than once (or more than a million times) in a free election? How can this be fair?

With Supreme Court justices appointed for life, how can they be held accountable to the interests of the larger population when they render decisions that can radically change the nature of our government?

A Supreme Court is a safeguard against the tyranny of a fifty-one percent majority and yet it appears that they can also become the representatives of the financial and power interests of the one percent at the top of the economic ladder. Should we be able to remove an offending justice without an impeachment trial through an occasional "re-appointment" based on past service?

During the summer months of 1787, delegates to Constitutional Convention met in Philadelphia to compose one of the most enduring documents of national governance ever written. This august body of white men said and did some amazingly insightful things, but at the bottom of that list is one sign of human frailty that we now call the "three-fifths compromise." Twenty-five of the fifty-five delegates to the Constitutional Convention were slave owners and the already hotly debated practice of slavery forced the delegates to come up with a way of counting the population in each state that accounted for the presence of these African slaves. The compromise they reached counted each black American as being three-fifths of a person.

This compromise is so embarrassing to our modern minds that when the newly elected Republican majority rose to read the Constitution aloud in the first session of Congress in January of 2011, they skipped this part. I was, however, reminded of the three-fifths rule when the Supreme Court announced its decision to lift the limits on individual political contributions.

What meager restrictions there were to limit the influence of political donations in our election process had been put in place following the Watergate scandal to help restore the confidence of average Americans in how our democracy was being managed. The five Republican-appointed members of the Supreme Court felt that limiting political donations to $75,000 was an unconstitutional limit to "free speech." Of course, a $75,000 cap was inhibiting no average American, nor would many have been much affected by a $75 cap. But in the world of politics, as Justice Antonin Scalia said regarding the McCutcheon vs. FEC ruling that lifts that donation aggregate ceiling from $75,000 to $3.5 million, "I don't think that $3.5 million is a heck of a lot of money."[1]

So, if, in a fit of enthusiasm for Elizabeth Warren's never materializing presidential campaign, I manage to donate $100, and a wealthy advocate for her opponent can donate $3.5 million, then my "freedom of speech" in affecting the next election is not three-fifths of a wealthy donor's. If, as the Supreme Court has insisted, "money is speech," then a wealthy donor has as much speech as approximately a half million average citizens who can make only a modest contribution (if any) to political campaigns. If you are starting to cynically conclude that your vote doesn't really count, then you are getting the message that the Supreme Court is trying to send to you. Rich people own and run the country so please keep your opinions to yourselves.

It gets worse. The $3.5 million cap is just for an individual candidate and there are ways around that. You can donate to a political party, to political action committees, and to issue-related committees. Someone like the Vegas casino owner, Sheldon Adelson, who donated $93 million in the 2012 election cycle, has more voice than millions of people like you and

1. Levinson, "Supreme Court ruling: As if we don't have enough money in politics already."

like me. Is that democracy? Is this kind of homage to the aristocracy what we get from the Tea Party conservatives who say that they want to take our country back? Why do they want it back if they are only going to destroy democracy and set up an oligarchy based on wealth?

The Creative Memory of Those on the Wrong Side of History

Most nations seem to have difficulty being self-critical about important decisions made in history. Americans are now generally willing to acknowledge the sins of slavery and the ethnic cleansing carried out against American Indian tribes, though we still seem to resist acknowledging how much of northern Mexico that we turned into the American southwest at the tip of a bayonet. What do you believe to have been America's most tragically immoral decisions in your lifetime?

President Kennedy was regarded well by history for avoiding a shooting war with the Soviet Union during the Cuban Missile Crisis, but can you see President Obama receiving similar treatment for choosing to negotiate a limited nuclear treaty with Iran rather than going to war, as many right wing politicians seemed to prefer?

Since it now appears to be evident that George W. Bush administration's decision to invade Iraq was sold to Congress with intentionally false information, why have former president Bush and former vice-president Cheney never been put on trial for treason or war crimes?

There are a few highly recognizable and deeply embarrassing moments in history when someone made a bold decision that was later revealed to have been horribly wrong. Think of George Wallace standing in front of Foster Auditorium at the University of Alabama on June 11, 1963 to prevent the integration of that university. Or remember that pained and embarrassed look on General Colin Powell's face when he testified before the United Nations on February 5, 2003 as he assured the world that Iraq had weapons of mass destruction and was manufacturing more in mobile labs built into trucks that didn't exist and had never been seen by anyone. I'm sure that George Wallace did some good things in office, but all I remember him for was his adamant promise "Segregation now, segregation tomorrow, segregation forever."

I know that Colin Powell was a highly accomplished military and political leader but, wittingly or unwittingly, he played a major role in starting an illegal war resulting in the deaths of hundreds of thousands of innocent civilians and wrecking the economy of the world. His legacy is forever marred for not standing up to Bush and Cheney in their malevolent plan. Still, when I heard him speak at a local university, he described his role in history in almost messianic intonations without the slightest hint of apology for having facilitated one of Americas most heinous wars.

Legacy stared the nine justices of the United States Supreme Court in the face in the spring of 2015. The great American sexual apartheid, bolstered by a generation of misinformation and prejudiced political stump speeches, largely from Republican candidates but helped by evangelicals and Roman Catholic clergy, was facing its inevitable end. There really was no rational way of stopping the advance of equal rights for gay couples in America. The only question before them that spring was whether they would hold open the door to an inevitable ethical awakening or forever be derided for trying to block the doorway of justice?

High court watchers speculated that it was an awareness of legacy that made Chief Justice Roberts cast the deciding vote that allowed the Affordable Care Act to stand, especially following the disastrous decision to allow unlimited corporate money to influence elections in the Citizens United case in which the court ruled that corporations are people.

Let's be honest, making a decision about same-sex marriage had little or nothing to do with the actual job of the Supreme Court in interpreting the Constitution. The unavoidable issue here is that it fell to the judiciary to interpret the constitution in a way that helped the United States to arrive at a final decision on a social institution, marriage, that the authors of the Constitution would never have considered.

There are five justices appointed by Republican presidents for their conservative bona fides and it was almost certain that at least four of them would vote against allowing full and equal rights for gay couples. I could not quite bring myself to believe that Chief Justice Roberts would allow history to come down the tracks and run him over, leaving him a legacy of ignorant prejudice, but, in the end, he surprised me and voted against expanding the right for same-sex couples to marry in all fifty states in the Obergefell v. Hodges ruling in June of 2015. In the end, Roberts left it to Reagan appointee, Anthony Kennedy, to break with the Republican appointed block of justices to vote with the four justices appointed by presidents Clinton and Obama.

Roberts may not retire in my lifetime but if he does and he hits the lucrative speaking tour, I'll be sure to go to hear him say, "Some of my best friends are gay."

The Right Stuff to Run a Country

> In almost every case, the candidate with the largest "war chest" going into an election will win. If that is true, is it the fault of voters or the fault of political donation rules that allows unqualified candidates to gain seats in our House of Representatives?
>
> Do you believe that there should be minimum educational requirements to be a candidate for federal office or at least the ability to pass a detailed civics test that would assure voters that a candidate understands how the American government works?
>
> You cannot be a medical doctor, or a licensed attorney, or (in most denominations) even a member of clergy, without first earning a graduate degree in your area of professional studies and passing an entrance exam. Why would we expect less of members of Congress?

Allow me to pose a hypothetical: Suppose that our government was largely managed by 435 professionals charged with overseeing the federal budget, military, transportation, food safety, foreign affairs, etc. And let's say that different regions of the country were allowed to select someone from their area to appoint to this management body. What kind of qualifications would we want our applicants to have? Surely we would choose a qualified individual from among experienced political science professors, accountants, attorneys, and administrators. As we looked through resumes, we would certainly discard candidates who did not have exemplary experience and education.

We would not, if the selection were based on qualifications, hire someone who made low grades in school before dropping out, or someone with no relevant experience to fill that coveted spot allotted to represent any region of the country. However, since our hypothetical is, in fact, the reality of our elected Congress and in the Congressional district where I live, we did, in fact, fill our seat with a college dropout with no relevant skills or experience, we are left to wonder why 63 percent of my neighbors in the Ozarks voted for someone you would not hire to manage a shoe store at the mall.

Why, from among the 300,000 people in this district, didn't we choose someone with outstanding qualifications? Clearly, our campaign donation driven election system is fatally flawed. Our nation's founders could never have foreseen the role of media advertising in elections, forcing both candidates and even elected officials to be perpetual fundraisers. In fact, two of the Tea Party's recently elected candidates, Reps. Pete Sessions of Texas and Mike Fitzpatrick of Pennsylvania, knew so little about what it meant to be a member of Congress that they actually missed being sworn in because they were already attending a fundraiser.

My Congress member, former real estate auctioneer, Billy Long, was elected on a river of campaign donations that largely came from outside of our state. Halliburton, Exxon, R. J. Reynolds, The American Bankers Association, as well as Mitt Romney, John Boehner, Eric Kantor, and Paul Ryan funded Long's election. There is no way to be elected or re-elected without major donors, so how independent is any member of Congress to actually represent his or her voters? Long's campaign slogan said that he was "fed up" with business as usual in Washington but his voting and campaign finance look like every other lobbyist-influenced career politician, demonstrating just how broken the system is.

The Federal Election Commission regulations form a readily available 244-page tome that, following the Supreme Court's decision allowing unfettered corporation donations to Super PACs, have diminished the importance of voters and increased the role of donations, and now the donors are anonymous! We have created a political system that favors the wealthy and diminishes the voice of the people.

Nothing is more vital to our political future than massive campaign finance reform. However, the corporations that control our government are not likely to allow us to amend the rules. Our freedom has been sold and it is unclear how we might get it back without a revolution.

Pretending To Fix the Federal Budget

Congress writes a federal budget of $3.5 trillion per year almost 70 percent of which goes to Social Security, Defense, and Medicare. We cannot mathematically balance the federal budget without addressing these three major arenas of spending. Where would you cut first?

Simply raising the income level cut-off could save social security solvency. Why are higher income earners protected from Social Security tax on earnings over $120,000 per year?

Allowing the system to competitively bid for prescription drugs could dramatically cut Medicare expenditures. Why is it important to protect the pharmaceutical industry profits at the expense of American tax-payers?

"Slick" Willie Sutton, was apocryphally reported to have answered the question, "Why do you rob banks?" by saying "Because that's where the money is." That's the kind of statement of the obvious that is missing from Congressional debates on the federal budget.

Deficit spending threatens our ability to retire at a reasonable age, to obtain necessary healthcare, to buy a house or send our kids to college. However, neither political party shows meaningful or sincere leadership in addressing our budget deficit.

Republicans often use any year's budget crisis to go after Planned Parenthood, National Public Radio, and the National Endowment for the Arts, furthering their reactionary social agenda but doing nothing about the deficit. This is maddeningly deceptive and irresponsible, but it doesn't put any roses in hand to throw at Democrats who went along with extending the Bush tax cuts, a move that accounts for two-thirds of our current deficit. The eight years of the Bush administration's tax cuts did not stimulate the economy, which was easily predictable.

The tax cuts did double our national debt and in the face of such a phenomenal disaster, President Obama agreed to extend them, cementing my cynicism about how much progressives can trust the Democratic Party. There is no way to avoid bankruptcy without addressing this welfare for the super-rich tax structure. Everyone in Congress knows this, but the majority is willing to trade our future for short-term political advantage.

But when it comes to cutting spending, the real money is only in three places: Social Security, defense, and Medicare. Social Security cannot reasonably be cut for low-income seniors though there are savings to be gained at the top if only Congress would have the courage to raise the income cutoff for top earners.

Paul Ryan's suggestion of cutting Medicare by giving seniors vouchers to buy health insurance amounts to asking low and middle-income seniors to do the public the favor of dying as soon as possible. It was yet another obscene attempt at moving more money into the hands of insurance companies while pointing seniors towards the graveyard.

We can dramatically reduce Medicare spending while expanding healthcare coverage if we had a Congress sufficiently courageous to stand up to insurance, pharmaceutical, and medical lobbies. The Republican Party is too deeply indebted to the aforementioned special interests to provide any leadership, but when the Democratic Party controlled both houses and the White House, they gave us a healthcare bill that once again reached into the pockets of Middle America to appease insurance companies.

The defense department is the real hole in the bottom of our financial boat. We fight unnecessary wars with price tags far larger than any possible accomplishments, and we maintain military bases around the world and a nuclear arsenal predicated on a Cold War that has been over since 1989. Homeland Security is now an unmanageable monolith, rivaling even the size of the Department of Education in the budget!

We must end our habit of military adventurism, close foreign military bases, cut Homeland Security, reduce the nuclear arsenal, and invest in education, transportation, alternative energy and infrastructure, but this is the message that is missing from both parties. America is waiting for real leadership.

Keeping Tea Safe for Twenty-First Century Americans

It is very difficult to change established bureaucracy. One way to eliminate unnecessary federal expenses would be to give the President of the United States the line-item veto crucial to most states' governors in balancing state budgets. To date, the Supreme Court has ruled the line item veto unconstitutional but if possible, would you grant this power to the office of the President?

Would you favor a first strike against rogue nations that are attempting to develop a nuclear weapon?

Why should the United States maintain a nuclear arsenal larger than what would be necessary to kill billions of people and to bring on a nuclear winter? Isn't that enough?

Two generations ago, when Richard Nixon was running for President, he derided wasteful government spending and used as the most absurd example the board of tea tasters paid by the US government to come to New York every year to sample tea imports since the late 1800s. He vowed to cut out wasteful federal spending and balance the budget. Of course, Nixon came and went, as did Ford, Carter, Reagan, Bush, Clinton, and "W," all of whom tried to cut funding for the tea tasting board, and yet we are still protected from bad tea by this federal program which we cannot seem to get rid of, even after nearly fifty years of trying.

For both Republicans and Democrats, bureaucracy is difficult or nearly impossible to change once a precedent of spending has been established. Of course, tea is not my real concern. I am anxious about Cold War spending which is now twenty years out of date and can only be corrected by decisive action in the Senate. We currently spend $55 billion every year just to maintain an aging nuclear arsenal that is twenty times larger than we could ever possibly use, even in an absolute nightmare scenario of a nuclear war.

There is a plausible reason for political debate here. Fiscally conservative Republicans might call for a $50 billion reduction in nuclear arms spending to reduce the deficit. Socially conscious Democrats might petition that the savings be diverted to something such as providing clean water in developing countries. In fact, I'll go ahead and start now: $50 billion dollars could provide clean drinking water to more than three hundred million people, which would do more to prevent future terrorist attacks than anything done to date by our aggressive military policy.

Scientists estimate that the detonation of fifty of our nuclear weapons would bring on a nuclear winter that would result in billions of deaths, which, by my calculation, should be more than enough. We presently maintain more than nine thousand nuclear weapons, the proliferation of which makes an accident or theft seem all too possible. Just fifty pounds of weapon grade nuclear material, in the wrong hands, could be put into a suitcase and could be used to flatten any city in the world.

Perfectly reasonable people can argue whether we should cut nuclear spending to reduce the deficit or to increase foreign aid, but no sane person can defend this level of spending on military hardware that has been virtually useless since 1989. Unfortunately, citizens have no direct vote on such specifics as the New START (Strategic Arms Reduction Treaty) or the nuclear non-proliferation agreement with Iran. Only in a political campaign can we address the need for transforming our defense department's budget and nuclear arsenal, a topic rarely mentioned in any campaign.

The State of the Union Address I Dreamed Of

> When the oil reserves of the Middle East are depleted or if the western world succeeds in shifting to alternative energy sources, what will sustain the nations currently dependent on oil revenue?

> If we closed most foreign military bases and reduced our military spending by 50 percent, what might we do with the resources of money, scientific intellect, and staff now consumed by our military?

> It might be too much to ask for us to imagine what Jesus might have done if he were the American president, but what if we had elected someone like Martin Luther King Jr. or Dorothy Day to the office of POTUS? What would his or her first State of the Union sound like?

Midway through his first term in office, as President Barack Obama rose to the podium to deliver one the most-watched State of the Union Addresses in American history I allowed myself to imagine the speech I wanted to hear him deliver. In my dreams, Obama said:

"Our policy of military engagement in a war on terror in the Middle East has been an economic, foreign policy, security, and moral failure. Consistent with every modern attempt at occupying and controlling the governments of the Middle East, our American adventurism has cost us thousands of lives, trillions of dollars and nearly all of our credibility, while not only failing to make us more safe, but in fact provoking new generations of terrorists. This absurd chapter of American history ends tonight.

The nations of the Middle East face a daunting future as their own reserves of oil are rapidly being depleted while their populations are growing unsustainably. Americans will move to cease all military involvement in foreign nations and will devote our scientific and economic resources to the development of the energy sources and means of transportation of the future, rather than continuing to race toward ruin from the gas-powered economy of the past century. The Arab world must now make immediate plans for self-government and a future beyond American oil revenues.

Domestically we have seen the final culmination of successive conservative appointments to the Supreme Court in their decision to remove all restrictions from corporate campaign contributions. Our democratic form of government has been under assault from powerful special interests for more than half a century. The retirement of Justice Sandra Day O'Connor saw the end of any check on the Supreme Court's agenda of giving America away to large corporations and now we must take every measure necessary to reclaim both our nation and our highest court. Tomorrow I will seek to work with this Congress on drafting a Constitutional Amendment that will cement campaign finance reform in a way that will restore the authority of voters to elect their government.

It was President Reagan who last articulated the management of this nation as a "trickle-down" economy. Clearly, as his own staff described it, this approach is nothing but a Trojan horse for the poor. Each president since Reagan, whether Republican or Democrat, has essentially maintained this trickle-down philosophy, as the gap between the rich and the poor has widened and the access of working Americans to such basic aspirations as home ownership, higher education, and appropriate healthcare has become less and less. I realize that they only call it class warfare when the poor begin to fight back in an economic war that the rich have been waging against them for more than a century. We stand on the verge of an economic collapse that could lead to civil war if we do not take dramatic steps to strengthen America's middle class. Our economy can no longer be based on a constant state of war and it can no longer be a system rigged to serve only the rich."

He might have said more, but thunderous applause from the joint session of Congress joined with cheers from living rooms from coast to coast making it impossible for him to continue.

Where Is The Real Power That Governs The United States?

Does our current government retain the authority to accomplish the kind of substantive change we saw during the integration of public schools, the creation of the Environmental Protection Agency, and the creation of the interstate highway system (or even the WPA)?

Can we really claim to have a representative government in the presence of unlimited political donations from billionaires and corporations?

Should the United States consider holding a constitutional convention to create a parliamentary form of democracy?

A candidate for superintendent of schools in my hometown wisely asked for a provision in his contract that assured him the authority to do his job. Maybe it shouldn't have to be said, but the truth is that many executives are put into positions of visible leadership but they are not given the authority to actually do what they need to do.

Apparently, President Obama should have negotiated a similar clause in his job description. During the Bush years, when our nation's credibility and resources were being thrown away to fatten the coffers of military suppliers and the oil industry, it was easy to conclude that this disastrous economic and foreign policy was being generated by intellectual midgets and corrupt corporate power brokers.

Obama's election was a relief to people all over the world. At last, we believed, the United States will return to sanity with an administration filled with trustworthy and well-qualified appointments. Not to diminish the substantive accomplishments of the Obama administration, but for most of his tenure it has become evident that you can put a good man in the White House and very smart people in the administration and still not change much.

This is nowhere more evident than in the BP Gulf oil spill debacle. Obama's Energy Secretary, Steven Chu, is one of the smartest people in the world, holding both a PhD in physics and a Nobel Prize. He is just the person we need in the midst of our energy crisis. However, during a interview on MSNBC, he was asked why, since President Obama had declared a moratorium on deep water drilling, permits were still being issued for wells in even deeper water than the one which no one seemed to be able to stop from leaking crude oil at a rate of more than two million gallons per day. His answer: "All I know about it is what I have read in the New York Times." The guy who is supposed to be in charge was not even in the loop! No matter how many thousands of miles of coastline are contaminated and how much wildlife is killed, no one in government can stop the approval of drilling permits that the oil industry wants because, in a contest between big oil and the Federal government, oil seems to consistently win.

Similarly, the EPA told BP to stop using the chemical dispersant, Co-rexit, because it is a toxin whose impact on marine life is, well, toxic. BP, in spite of all its expensive ads and posturing, replied by saying, "No." And the EPA replied by saying, "OK, well then, try to use less Corexit." BP said, "Riiiiggghhtt!"

Now, it is helpful to note that BP does not use Corexit off the coast of Great Britain because the government there will not allow it to be used. Our government would like to make it illegal to use, but our government doesn't have that kind of power. Our visible government is increasingly nothing more than a sock-puppet providing cover for the real government that is comprised of oil, insurance, pharmaceutical and banking interests. And that, dear reader, is a bad thing.

The Government and Vital Industries

> Would you be willing to re-roof your house with white shingles if you knew it would save you $300 a year?

> Would you be willing to have a white roof if every other roof in your neighborhood was also white?

> Can we combine capitalism and socialism to create certain indus-tries to promote jobs and the common good such as the manufac-ture of solar panels, wind turbines, and energy saving appliances?

Major banks in the midst of our most recent recession were deemed to be "too big to fail," and the automobile industry seemed to squeak by in the same universe of for-profit industries believed to be important enough to save with public money.

When the housing market went through hard times in 2008, more than 800,000 jobs were lost in two years in the construction field alone. The housing bust and the fear in the business world about further capital invest-ment deeply wounded this vital portion of our economy. Federal bailouts and stimulus plans have taken the appearance of a "No Wealthy Banker Left Behind" program. Where is the stimulus/rescue plan for the thousands of people who used to feed their families and fuel the economy with their earnings gained at the end of a hammer and saw?

Carpenters, electricians, plumbers, roofers, and bricklayers are ulti-mately more crucial to economic recovery than propping up a bank on every street corner in every town. We should not see an economic crisis as if it is a stand-alone event. The ailing economy is complicated by energy and environmental crises at the same time. So far, it seems that government stimulus just takes us back into doing more of what created the energy and environment problems in the first place. Come on, politicians—we cannot fix the economy by doing more of what got us into trouble in the first place.

Here is my suggestion: Address all three issues simultaneously by investing in the creation of green jobs. Immediately put construction workers back on the job by giving tax incentives to businesses and homeowners to retrofit their buildings and houses with energy saving technologies. Give grants or low-interest business loans to startup companies with renewable energy inventions so that we can get away from oil and coal dependence. The good folks at the Center for American Progress have crunched the numbers.[2]

Eschewing the "Drill baby drill," mentality, if we invest $100 billion in green jobs rather than the same amount in oil we would see:

1. Four times more jobs being created and 300,000 more jobs than in simple tax refunds to households.

2. Create three times as many good jobs with salaries over $16 per hour.

3. Reduce the overall unemployment rate by more than 20 percent.

When Energy secretary Steven Chu said that painting your roof white could cut air conditioning costs by 15 percent late night comedians had a field day with it. However, scientists pointed out that if every house in America had a white roof it would reduce pollution by an amount equivalent to the exhaust of every automobile on the planet for eleven years. So, rather than laughing at the suggestion, why haven't we seen some enterprising business take hold of the idea and market white roofing materials?

Every homeowner has the option right now of replacing her or his hot water heater with an on-demand system that does not store hot water but heats it only when needed, resulting in a drastic cut in utilities while giving a never ending supply of hot water. Why hasn't our government offered a tax cut or a subsidy to help homeowners make this change?

"Change" should not be an election year mantra; it really needs to be a mandate.

2. Center for American Progress. "Green Recovery."

Public Transit and the Public Good

Do you know how to get from your home to your job on public transit? Have you ever done it?

Would you use public transit if it was safe, clean, and efficient?

How many cars does your family own now and how many would you own if you could use reliable local public transit? How much money would reducing the number of cars at your house save you annually?

I love to travel but I am terrified of driving in foreign countries. Fortunately, an English-speaking guy from rural America can fairly easily figure out how to get around in big American cities like New York and Chicago, as well as in London, and even in places where language is a barrier such as Paris, Rome, Athens, and Copenhagen.

Getting around town in my Missouri hometown using the public buses, however, is rather more challenging, even for those of us who live here. Most bus stops do not have bus schedules or routes posted. There are no buses for those who work past eleven p.m. If you have a job that requires Saturday or Sunday hours, it is much more difficult to travel by bus.

The city bus system is an albatross around City Utilities' neck. It loses money and has nothing to do with its mission of providing electricity, gas and water to the community. It was inherited from a previous age when the city's electric trolley system was the major user of electricity. The trolleys are long gone, so now CU finds itself in possession of a system on which it loses money every time someone steps onto a bus. CU has no motivation to make the bus system user-friendlier or to add routes and extend coverage.

Transportation is the largest hurdle in moving people from public assistance to work. Why are there illegal immigrants working in the hotels in the nearby entertainment mecca, Branson, Missouri? Because you can't take a bus the twenty-five miles from the larger city where I live, Springfield, Missouri, to Branson, and the jobs don't pay enough to buy a car and make the fifty-mile daily commute.

Sure, expanding bus service to outlying bedroom communities is expensive but calculate the expense of all those cars slowly inching along the major roads into and out of employment every day and factor in the environmental impact of that many motors running, waiting to push the empty seats of cars along those major arteries of my fair city and yours and you can quickly see that mass transit is the least expensive way to move people around town. Of course, having park-and-ride parking lots in those outlying communities also helps; they come with a price tag but they are working in the cities that have tried them. Why not build them before being driven to it by absolute necessity?

Walking is not much of an option when sidewalks do not connect residential areas to work areas. In many of our major cities including Dallas and Denver, where there is a large workforce who do not own cars, sidewalks are sporadic and do not provide a safe option to those who might walk to work. Biking isn't a safe option when cities just paint a bike lane by the curb of a street with fast-moving car traffic as is done in even infrastructure rich communities such as Boston. But visit a city like Copenhagen where even in the harsh Denmark winter the majority of the workforce either walks or rides bikes . . . because the city's infrastructure allows it.

It is in every city's interest to help the poor find work and make it to work on time. It is in every city's best interest to cut down on traffic congestion by making bus and train commuting more realistic and more attractive. It is, however, completely unrealistic to expect profit-driven industry to take on this expensive challenge. This is a problem that has been solved in cities all over the world and it is long past time for American cities to intelligently implement the best practices already in place in much of the developed world.

2

Elections

. . . voting for a Republican is like buying a lottery ticket. The lottery serves the interests of a very few people at the expense of millions of gullible ticket buyers who hope against hope (or who are being punished for not paying attention in math class) that they will become one of the rich few . . .

In the Twilight of Empire

Is it time to allow America's star to fade in the world or is it important for the United States to remain as the only global superpower?

The media rakes in huge profits from long political campaigns that spend hundreds of millions of dollars in each cycle. However, since the people own the airways, couldn't we require free political advertisements in exchange for the FCC licenses of radio and TV stations to limit the power of political donations?

Can anything short of a constitutional amendment place realistic limits on the length of political campaigns and the amount of money donated and spent in elections?

Empires rise and empires fall. How quickly they rise and how fast they fall depends on a number of factors. The shifting map of power and resources saw the United States of America become the dominant empire both as a result of the military advances of WWI and WWII and because of the innovation, invention and economic expansion that was rooted in the American genius and work ethic.

Many of our most important economic and scientific advances came to us through an immigrant population who came here, in large part, because there was sufficient freedom and opportunity here to allow genius to bloom and bear fruit. The torch of "the greatest nation on earth" is passing from our hands, not because we suddenly have a dearth of indigenous inventive genius, but because our political and economic system has become the opposite of what it was during America's ascendency.

While progressive nations are forging ahead in alternative power sources, we are doubling down on coal and oil. In expanding economies, national healthcare plays a huge role in allowing new entrepreneurs to leave their jobs to start new businesses without fear of losing their healthcare or being bankrupted by its cost and old successful businesses are not burdened by the benefits costs of a generation of retired employees. Nations that are moving into leadership in this century invest in the future of their nation through education, agriculture, and important infrastructure investments in mass transit while avoiding the expense of maintaining a bloated military. We are doing the opposite of everything that would keep us in a position of global leadership.

There are many factors involved in the self-destructive path we're following but the single most important one is our failure to address campaign finance reform. In fact, not only have we failed to take the same corrective measures seen in other developed nations, we have gone to great lengths to make it worse, as seen in the 2010 Supreme Court decision in the Citizens United case equating campaign donations with free speech.

The oil and coal lobby blocks any meaningful innovation in our power sources. Our healthcare costs have skyrocketed because of the political influence through campaign donations from medical interests. We have failed to develop our mass transit because of the political donations from road construction and automobile manufacturing lobbies. And the largest waste of all is in our astonishingly bloated and economically insane military spending, funded almost solely due to presence of political donations. Do we dare to call it bribery? If not, what is it?

Our elected officials are not inherently evil, nor are they universally ignorant, but they are the inferior product of a corrupt election process and the only way to keep America from diving into the sewer of modern history is to enact radical and sweeping campaign finance reform. Of course, the people who are getting very rich and the people who remain in government's seats of power will be devoted to the system that has blessed them while destroying our once great nation. The question that remains is whether American voters can find the will to change this course before it is too late.

Would the Real Republicans Please Stand Up?

> Even the most enthusiastic of Democrats would not argue for a single party political system but it seems that the Republican Party has abandoned its core principles. Today, would anyone vote for a genuinely economically responsible Republican who did not marry his or her economic conservatism to corporatism and social conservatism?
>
> Will the religious right continue to be able to influence elections in the next decade?
>
> Would you consider a change to a parliamentary form of government in the United States?

The Moral Majority came on the political scene during the presidential election of 1980. Their anti-abortion message evolved over the next decade into anti-gay hysteria as the world became aware of the threat of AIDS. Various organizations have risen and dispersed over the past 30 years, but the political energy of the religious right has remained constant.

Those of us who have observed the news for a couple of generations are aware that for most of this time the moralizing has been largely symbolic. Ronald Reagan no more intended to make abortion illegal than he could simultaneously cut taxes, balance the budget, and increase military spending as he promised. Anyone with a double digit IQ could easily see that it was mathematically impossible to do these things at the same time, but it motivated the unaware. The moral drum beat is intended to get religious people to vote for a party that economically exploits them while promising to legislate the impossible—or did anyone really believe that making homosexuality illegal will turn gay people straight? If politicians promised to make salads taste like chocolate pie would you believe them?

The problem with the Moral Majority's latest incarnation, the Tea Party, is that it may actually believe its own slogans. They really do want to persecute people for being gay. They really do want to regulate women's reproductive lives. They really do believe that they can control people's thoughts and beliefs through oppressive government action. It used to be simply symbolic rhetoric aimed at the gullible, but now we have a real flesh and blood politicians, such as Missouri's infamous Todd Akin, who actually believe that women don't get pregnant from being raped and enough idealists like Paul Ryan to produce a Republican Party Platform that actually insists on the victims of rape giving birth to any child conceived by rape.

It was sad that politicians found so many people vulnerable to manipulation in the past, but now it is frightening that their decades of rhetoric is turning into an actual agenda. The clowns are running the Republican circus and there seems to be no hope of a return to rational Republican strong defense, economic conservative values without this inexcusable anti-women, anti-gay, anti-poor, anti-sick, anti-elderly, anti-education, anti-environment, and anti-children agenda coming with it.

I am a social liberal but an economic conservative. I believe that we need a viable two party system that works for compromises aimed at providing a real safety net for the vulnerable while rationally managing a federal budget that fosters a healthy business environment and a responsible citizenry.

I have often voted for local Republicans who advocated for economic realism, but national politicians whose unwavering loyalty to pharmaceutical and tobacco interests are entirely untenable to me. Please, would the real Republicans, the rational, intelligent, economic conservative, and sanely motivated people please reclaim your party!

Who Chooses the Next President?

> How "pure" is your own voting history? Could you reasonably be called a "swing" voter?
>
> If you consistently vote for candidates of one party, can you articulate the reasons for your voting loyalty?
>
> Is our long history of having only two viable parties in contention for our nation's highest office serving our nation's best interests?

One of the most frustrating things about a presidential election is that all political ads, debates and robo-calls are really aimed at a small fraction of the population. In our evenly divided electorate, about 48 percent are going to vote for the Democratic nominee and another 48 percent are going to vote for the Republican, not out of party loyalty or ideological purity, but because those who are concerned about social programs are never likely to vote for a Republican and the anti-tax, pro-military, pro-corporate, anti-healthcare, anti-gay voters are not likely to ever vote for a Democrat.

That leaves the selection of our nation's future president to a thin slice of the voting public who are called simply "undecided," but I wonder what other adjectives could be used to describe these one in twenty-five citizens? A Pew Research survey found the majority of undecided voters to be female, over the age of 65, and they tended to be less educated and more religious than the mainstream voters.[1] As long as that description remains accurate to describe the real deciders in presidential elections it doesn't bode well for progressive candidates, which makes me feel what Winston Churchill felt when he said, "The best argument against democracy is a five minute conversation with the average voter."

When you consider the fact that the majority of Americans either do not believe in evolution (43 percent) or are not sure (16 percent)[2] you may begin to think that Thomas Jefferson was onto something when he suggested that only a certain portion of the population should be allowed to vote. We would vehemently disagree with his choice of white, male landowners, but we ought to be able to weed out the flat earth society.

Plato's laudatory description of a republic left government in the hands of a few trustworthy leaders (philosopher-kings). I wonder what the Greek sage would say about our republic, which has now evolved to put our most crucial decision into the hands of a minority whose sole qualification is that after nearly fifty years of voting, they can't decide which set of priorities are the most important to them until Election Day?

With the Republican attacks on gay marriage, access to contraception, Planned Parenthood, social services, and immigrants, and their constant defense of tax relief for the super-rich, you might think that the people who are willing to cast a vote for any Republican could meet in a phone booth. It isn't just that it is difficult to imagine a woman, a person of color, or a gay person voting Republican, but even we white, male, heterosexuals who happen to know and care about the interests of women, gays, and minorities wouldn't do so either. And yet, our nation stands divided, 48 percent to 48 percent waiting to see which candidate the undecided will decide upon.

1. NPR, "Who Are the Undecided Voters?"

2. Huffington Post, "Obama Muslim Rumors Persist Among Illinois Republicans: 39 Percent Believe President Is Muslim."

The One with the Most Gold Makes the Rules

> Do you believe that either of the grassroots movements of Occupy Wall Street or the Tea Party influenced the elections of 2012?
>
> Does the Iowa Caucus give disproportionate importance to candidates favored by politically and religiously conservative, white voters?
>
> The largest corporate donors to presidential elections donate in fairly equal amounts to both candidates. Does this mean that these top donors are going to be treated equally favorably by either party?

The Iowa Caucuses are primarily interesting because they are the first volley in a presidential primary season. Many journalists have commented on how irrelevant the caucuses really are since Iowa, being so white, and conservative, is not representative of the nation. However, at least in the 2012 election cycle, Iowans did speak for all of us in one important way: they did not seem to care much for the field of candidates.

There was a tremendous amount of dissatisfaction and agitation among American voters that year, and I am inclined to see both the Tea Party and the Occupy Wall Street crowds, though ideologically at opposite ends of the political spectrum, as having been provoked by similar issues. The Tea Party was eventually co-opted to be an ultra-conservative wing of the Republican Party but it didn't start out that way, just as Democrats tried their best to recruit the Occupy movement even though they clearly rejected both parties and eventually disappeared from the scene.

Our nation really is in trouble. There is no logical way to deny the fact that the growing income gap between the rich and the working class will destroy our democracy. But, like a pickpocket that distracts your attention while stealing your wallet, both Republicans and Democrats keep trying to get us to believe that the solution to this path towards annihilation lies in voting for them rather than the other guy, while both accept political donations from the institutions that are fueling the class disparity.

A cursory look at our election system reveals two inevitable facts: the candidate with the largest campaign fund wins 94 percent of the time and the largest donors to both parties tend to be the same corporations. Among the top donors to both Obama's and McCain's 2008 campaign were Citigroup, Goldman Sachs, JP Morgan Chase, Morgan Stanley and UBS AG.

If you have studied the international economic meltdown of the past few years it is not difficult to see that the engineers of the deadly transfer of wealth into the hands of the super-rich and the people who own and operate our elected officials through campaign contributions are these same corporations.

We continue to spend more on our military than the combined total of military spending in the rest of the world while insisting that we cannot afford to rebuild the infrastructure of our nation, provide healthcare to the sick, and education to our coming generation of wealth creators. Without infrastructure, education and healthcare, our defense department will shortly have no country left to defend but if our only option to correct this downward spiral is to vote for a different set of corporate sponsored politicians, there is no reason to believe that anything will change. As much as the conservative talking heads have despised President Obama, his actual actions in office have hardly differed from the administration of Ronald Reagan, not in what he says but in what he does, which is obviously what really matters.

I am sadly left to quote Lily Tomlin who once said, "No matter how cynical I get, I just can't keep up."

An Honest Politician

After the horrors of the Nazi takeover of the German government, post war Germany made it illegal for any politician to knowingly lie in a political campaign. Would it be too farfetched to suggest a jail sentence for intentional deception in American political campaigns?

Though there has been a lot of talk about campaign finance reform, the truth is that the past decade has seen us move dramatically backward in the way we fund our campaigns, allowing a very small number of super wealthy donors not only to choose our candidates but to also set the agenda for a campaign. Can we transition to a publicly funded election system that makes political donations illegal?

Is politics inherently corrupt or is it possible to enact ethical standards that can be meaningfully enforced?

In my first year of college I changed my major to philosophy even though I had received a bad grade on my first philosophy paper. It was, perhaps, the bad grade that drew me even deeper into my introductory course in philosophical problem solving. I went in to visit with my professor whose parents had, with a cruel lack of imagination, named Robert when their family name is Roberts. Perhaps that name made him impatient with the world in the way that naming a boy "Sue" is said to make a man tough. He said tersely, "Philosophy is about the search for the truth, not a contest to see who can debate the loudest." Robert Roberts graded and taught as if he meant for us to be passionate about the truth and dispassionate about argumentation.

One makes progress in the study of philosophy through the dialogues of Plato into the more meaty writings of Aristotle, Hume, Locke, and finally into the modern existentialist thinkers: Kierkegaard, Hegel, and Sartre. What is present in each is an increasingly methodic and dedicated search for what is true. That passion for truth, a friend recently wrote to me, is what is missing from our political dialogue as a whole.

Meaningful conversation dies when a national political figure such as Sarah Palin, is willing to allege that President Obama wants to install "death panels" to decide if people like her aging parents or her Down Syndrome affected child should live or die. Such blatant dishonesty not only does not further the public debate on healthcare, it brings the conversation to a halt, dividing the nation between those who want to improve the nation's healthcare and those who are cowering in fear of a Big Brother euthanasia program. Rather than responsibly repudiating this sad fear mongering propaganda, Iowa Senator Chuck Grassley actually repeated the slander!

Add to that the support given to the embarrassingly misguided birther movement by several members of Congress and the Senate, and one is left to wonder if the Republican Party has generally come to assume that misinformation is as effective as their standard fear mongering propaganda? Even though I am left-leaning in my politics, I take no delight in watching the Republican Party commit credibility suicide. While I acknowledge a wealth of examples of disappointing Democratic "pants on fire" public statements, the two parties cannot be said to be equally at fault. We need two honorable parties to keep our democracy strong. On the current political horizon there are no alternatives to the Republican Party other than the Democrats and yet the Republicans are moving decidedly in the direction of alienating voters who have critical thinking skills.

Though I am progressive in social justice issues, I might be inclined to vote for an economic conservative if the Republicans could find one who didn't try to use fear and misinformation to manipulate voters. Our democracy depends upon having a real choice of legitimate candidates who are capable of an intelligent, honest search for the truth.

As much as I would like to see civil dialogue replace the kind of disruptive hooliganism we've seen in political town hall meetings and primary candidate forums, it seems clear that what we can look forward to is a manipulative search for votes rather than a sincere search for the truth.

Poor and Minority Voters

Comedian Bill Maher has objected to calls for everyone to vote. He says that if you are not informed on the candidates and issues, "please stay home." Is he right? Is it possible that low voter turnout is a good thing?

If we believe in democracy, why wouldn't we make voting easier? Should we make Election Day a national holiday or move it to a weekend day?

British comedian Russell Brand advises against voting because it gives the deceptive sense that we actually have a decision-making role in government. He advocates for revolution rather than voting. Does voting really matter?

ACORN (Association of Community Organizations for Reform Now) is no more. They closed their doors in 2010 after an exposé that showed an employee giving advice to a couple asking for help in hiding their imaginary prostitution business from detection and taxation. Prior to that, ACORN, a federally funded agency, was active in community organizing and voter registration among poor and moderate-income neighborhoods.

The video exposé of that infamous conversation about how to protect sex-worker income from taxation turned being associated with ACORN into a kind of political poison. Politicians who had previously worked with ACORN because of their advocacy for the poor in matters of housing, wages, safety, healthcare, and voter's rights, suddenly had to bury any history of collaboration with the humiliated agency.

The ACORN employee who failed to negatively react to the reporters posing as a prostitution business was certainly in the wrong, but what about those 40 years of registering minority voters, helping people through the paper work to apply for public housing or for a better job? Surely we still need those services, unless, of course, you are opposed to trying to elevate the standard of living of the poor and you are especially opposed to the poor finding their way into the voting booth.

In our two party system, the most simple division of the parties is that the Republican party represents the economic interests of business owners, employers, and the wealthy, a far smaller population than the poor, unemployed, under employed, and voiceless, most commonly associated with the Democratic party. It is then, in the Republican Party's best interest to prevent the poor from voting whenever possible.

The demise of ACORN has no impact on sex workers not paying taxes on their income but it does successfully repress probable Democratic votes. But if a single embarrassing incident from a small office in ACORN can have such a huge impact, what would happen if we used similar public events to shame the Republican Party?

I have wanted to ask party officials why Republicans are in favor of gang-rape. That's right, legislation introduced by Senator Al Franken sought to end the practice of giving federal contracts to corporations that require their employees not to file charges against other employees for sexual assault. The legislation was prompted by the case of Jamie Lee Jones who was gang-raped in Iraq by her fellow Halliburton and KBR employees. The assailants then locked her in a container for a day to prevent her from reporting the incident. Of course, Halliburton/KBR required new employees to sign away their rights to file criminal charges in such cases, complicating Jones's case.

While the Franken anti-rape legislation did pass, 30 Republican senators voted against it! Every one of those senators should have been immediately handcuffed and put on trial for conspiracy in this gang-rape incident. So, Mr. Party Chairman, why do Republicans favor gang- rape? Isn't your opposition to ACORN really all about not wanting poor people to vote?

What does it say about your real devotion to democracy if you want to limit the percentage of the population who participates in democracy at the voting booth? And why worry about the minor infractions of an organization like ACORN when you are not worried about the fact that 75 percent of all elected Republican senators voted to protect Halliburton from liability in the gang-rape of its employees, a real crime which really happened to a real person? Why can't Republicans ever stand up to Halliburton or other campaign donors?

The Best Judiciary Money Can Buy

> Since Supreme Court justices so frequently vote as a block depending upon the political party of the president who appointed them, can we claim that our justices are nonpartisan?
>
> Is the life appointment of Supreme Court Justices one of the eighteenth-century aspects of our constitution that needs to be changed? If so, should it be a term of office or include a mandatory retirement age?
>
> If we were writing the constitution today, would we create a Supreme Court that is elected or appointed?

The greatest threats to the future of our delicate democracy are the level of influence political contributions and political advertising has on how our elected officials are chosen (and re-elected since, apparently, getting re-elected is the first priority of nearly every political office holder) and how our government makes decisions about which companies are awarded contracts for everything from roads to bombers. The influence of lobbyists, special interest money, political PACs, and corporations is taking away the ability of the United States government to operate by the people and for the people.

We news junkies get a lot more face time with our members of congress and our President than we get with the nine members of that more mysterious club which is the Supreme Court. However, just because their work is more shrouded in complexity and the slow process of decision-making does not mean that they are not just as "in it up to their eyebrows" as those politicians we elect. The flagrant refusal of Justice Thomas to recuse himself from cases involving the Affordable Care Act when his wife, Ginni, is employed by a Tea Party political action group that has actively opposed the ACA is only one example of a court run without a proper conscience.

American Presidents are in a unique position to extend their political agenda far into the future by appointing Supreme Court justices who can, in virtual seclusion, carry out heavy handed political agendas. We have seen the conservative majority of the Supreme Court blatantly dismantling a century of decisions that were intended to protect the integrity of our democratic political processes.

Though Republicans are usually the ones screaming about "activist judges" there are no judges more "activist" than our current Republican appointees, Samuel Alito and John Roberts who have been able to join with Anthony Kennedy and Clarence Thomas to undo past decisions without even a ghost of reason for reviewing these cases.

The Citizens United decision has taken the lid off corporate sponsorship of political ads overturning a decision made in 1907 that had been upheld in 2003. The only reason the Supreme Court can give to justify reviewing a previous decision is if circumstances of the case have substantially changed. The only thing that has changed since 2003 regarding corporations' involvement in politics is that the Republicans now have a judiciary willing to throw our political system down the toilet in order to give more power to their corporate donors. (Shamelessly, Justice Kennedy, who had written the minority opinion in 2003, simply dusted off his previous work and edited it to be the majority opinion in this case.) Now, for example, a foreign corporation can surreptitiously buy air time to oppose one candidate and promote another on the eve of an important election, virtually buying our government which Justices Roberts, Kennedy, Scalia, Alito, and Thomas were all too eager to sell.

The hypocritical defense of this horrible activist ruling was that it is a matter of free speech! But corporations are not people! The bill of rights wasn't written to protect corporations; it was written to protect citizens. Now, who will protect the citizens from the monarchical Republican judges?

When Voting Is Like Spitting Into the Wind

> Do you believe that lobbyist political donations can trump a majority vote in your state?

> Might it be possible, in our Internet age, to run our governments by direct democracy rather than by a representative form of government?

> When a referendum has been put to a public vote, shouldn't it require another pubic vote to resend the measure?

Most of my adult life has been lived in Missouri though when I get disgusted with Missouri politics I have only to wait a few days until I hear a story from my native Kentucky or our neighboring states of Arkansas, Kansas, and Oklahoma to realize that this is not the most intellectually challenged state in the country. There are, after all, Texas, Florida, Alabama, and Mississippi to also be considered. Still, if only Emma Goldman had lived long enough to see recent Missouri politics she would have all the proof she needed to support her view that, "If voting changed anything, they'd make it illegal."

It's not that the Missouri legislature has anything against the public voting on topics of great importance, as long as they can ignore those votes when their lobbyists find the voting public to be something of a nuisance. Yes, Missouri is one of the few states in America where a public vote can be virtually ignored by a vote of the legislature. If you were thinking of moving here . . . keep thinking.

In 1998 the NRA formed the ironically-named Missourians Against Crime to sponsor a statewide referendum to make it possible for gun owners to obtain a "conceal and carry" permit. Since the United States already has the highest gun fatality rate in the world, the citizens of Missouri wisely defeated this insane proposal in 1999. Faced with the choice of either honoring the votes of citizens or the political contributions of the NRA, our state legislature overturned that vote in 2003 and have since sought to further liberalize the conceal and carry laws to lower the age requirements and to extend the right to carry a concealed weapon onto college campuses and into the state capital building during legislative sessions. What could possibly go wrong?

More recently, after a great deal of public campaigning and demonstrations, the state voted to set tight restrictions on puppy mills which had previously flourished in our state because of the lack of regulation. However, while the ballots were still warm, the state senate decided that the voters didn't know much about animal abuse and they passed a bill that once again set aside the decision of voters.

In 2006 Missouri voters approved a very intelligent law that pegged the minimum wage to the cost of living. Again, members of the Missouri legislature assumed that voters didn't know much about business and poverty so they sought to reject the will of the voters. This was going to be an ugly battle so Senator Jane Cunningham stepped back from her proposal to do away with not only our minimum wage laws but our child labor protections as well but not because she had a genuine change of heart. She simply found another method to accomplish the same goal—that is by striking from the state budget any enforcement dollars to follow up on the hundreds of complaints made every year regarding child labor and minimum wage violations.

I don't know if any of our troops currently stationed abroad helping to birth democracy in the Middle East could possibly be re-deployed to Missouri, but it does seem that there is some need for a little help in getting our legislature to understand the basic principles of democracy, the first being that the will of the public expressed in the ballot box should be viewed as something sacred.

What the Missouri legislature has said loud and clear to Missouri voters is that they hold our views in disdain. I think we should return the favor when they are up for re-election.

Why Do So Many of the 99 Percent Vote against Themselves?

> Given that the democratic socialist governments in Western Europe have managed to solve many of the most vexing problems of poverty we experience in the United States, why do socialist ideas have such a bad reputation in the United States?
>
> Is the claim that both Democrats and Republicans essentially serve the interests of corporations and the wealthiest sufficient reason to advocate for new political parties in American politics?
>
> Do you feel that your own values and beliefs are represented by the choices you are given in the voting booth on election days?

I can speak as one disenfranchised Democratic voter: In fact, I have begun to tell my friends that I represent the Democratic wing of the Democratic Party. I couldn't believe my ears, after so many of us had worked so hard to elect our nation's first black president, when I heard that Obama had invited homophobic pastor, Rick Warren, to pray at his first inauguration. I was more disappointed when Obama responded to the negative reaction of his supporters by creating a second tier event at which the openly gay Episcopal Bishop, Gene Robinson, was allowed to take the stage, as if progressive voters were too stupid to recognize when we are being patronized.

Obama lost even more credibility with me when he told Mexican president Felipe Calderón that, though it should be done, it would take too much political capital to outlaw the sale of semi-automatic rifles in the U. S. even though our Wal-Mart stores in Texas are supplying the drug cartels in

Mexico with a tidal wave of lethal weapons. Caving into the NRA crowd, as if Obama had a snowball's chance in a place of eternal punishment of ever getting their support on anything, was just too morally puny to overlook.

Add to that his embarrassingly timid leadership in healthcare reform and a mind numbing pro-war speech in Oslo as he was awarded the Nobel Peace Prize and I can say that I am at the head of the line of progressives who are disappointed in President Obama. However, that disillusionment is not going to make me vote Republican.

One can understand why the super wealthy vote for a party that gives them, simultaneously, huge tax cuts and outrageous no-bid government contracts, but 99 out of every 100 Republican votes are cast by people who are shooting themselves in the foot in the infinitesimally small hope that they too may one day be among the financial elite of the nation.

Here in the Midwest, our Republican Senators and members of Congress leave us no reason to doubt the old proverb that says that politicians are interested in us in the same way that fleas are interested in dogs.

To Vote or Not to Vote? That's Not a Good Question!

> What do you think about compulsory voting as practiced in Australia, where, if you fail to vote, you may have to pay a fine?

> The state of Oregon became the first state to automatically register voters. Citizens can unregister themselves, but unless they take direct action, the voter's registration is automatic. Should this low-threshold approach be used to increase voter rolls nationwide?

> Should a state allow a business such as payday loan and title loan businesses to exist? Since no one is forced to use their services and hence pay their exorbitant interest rate, is the state obligated to protect people who won't protect themselves?

Low voter turnout for municipal elections has made some wonder if we should reconsider the nonpartisan elections most cities hold for council seats, judges, school board, and the mayor's office. It is certainly true that political parties do a good job of mobilizing voters, but before we jump in the direction of partisan elections, let me tell you about how our two party system is affecting the operation of the state where I live.

The idealistic goal of having two parties who send their best and brightest candidates to the legislature so that they will intelligently debate the issues and arrive at compromise policies that serve the best interests of the people in both parties is not at all what is happening in Washington, D.C. and we are certainly not seeing anything better in Jefferson City, Missouri. What we are getting from our divided house at both the federal and at many state houses are nearly straight party votes, often in total denial of information or intelligent debate.

If you live in a state that has not passed reasonable controls on predatory loans, please consider getting involved. If all affected states could pass regulations, such as have passed in other states, to cap interest rates at some sane point, say 36 percent APR rather than the 400 percent to 1900 percent currently being charged to the poor where I live, then I am confident that the general voting public would pass the measure by a huge majority. In my state, the proposed bill that would close the loophole that allows these predatory lenders to continue to prey on the desperately poor will never see the light of day as long as Republicans hold a majority in the house and senate.

In every legislative session in Missouri there are ten times more pieces of legislation proposed than will ever be voted on. Because of this overwhelming number of bills the legislature depends on a committee system to decide which ones get a chance to stand for a vote. The majority party appoints the committee chairs and if they choose to play dirty, and this Republican dominated legislature certainly does, no Democratically authored bill has much chance of getting to a floor vote.

Millions of people all across the United States are being fleeced by predatory lenders, and the only thing keeping them in business is the lack of legislative will to act on behalf of the vulnerable poor.

The Revolving Door of Legislators and Lobbyists

> Should former elected officials be able to accept jobs in the industries they had regulated or with whom they had negotiated procurement contracts while they were in office?

> Is it ethical for an elected official, once out of office, to leverage her or his working relationships with other elected officials as a paid lobbyist?

Do lobbyists play a necessary role in informing legislators and helping to shape legislation? Would our government be hurt if lobbying itself were outlawed?

If I ever had the chance to be one of the people asking presidential candidates questions in a pre-election town hall, I have my question ready. "In light of how much good Jimmy Carter has done since leaving the White House, what would you, (any candidate for POTUS), do with your notoriety and influence when your time in office is over?" I think the question goes to character. If being president makes you internationally famous and holds doors open to influence the world for the better, why would I ever vote for someone who didn't want to use that most favored status?

I have little chance of being in a position to pose any question to a presidential candidate, although I have raised this issue of public influence once out of office to candidates for the Congress and the Senate. Depending upon their committee assignments, members of congress can do a lot of favors for the industries that do business with the government and with those who are closely regulated by the government.

One of our Missouri senators has received large campaign contributions from the pharmaceutical industry. He has also been one of their best friends in making certain that their obscene profits are never challenged with such obviously logical things as allowing Medicare to competitively bid out their drug purchases. I would love to believe that there was no connection between campaign donations and this irrational defense of corporate profits, but I cannot muster any cynicism about the causal link here.

In one of my newspaper columns during a particularly close re-election campaign, I asked our senator: If you lose your bid to return to the Senate next fall will you make a pledge, right now, that you will not then take a job as a lobbyist for the insurance or pharmaceutical industry (or tobacco or the NRA)?

I explained, "I have to tell you, Senator Blunt, in the years that you have been in office, it sure does look like you have championed the causes of these special interests with an inexplicable deference. But that is a serious allegation and I would not say such a thing lightly. However, you can help to allay the appearance of an unholy alliance between you and these major contributors to your recent campaigns by publicly nailing shut any backdoor option to make millions of dollars in reward for your loyalty to these industries over these past years." Senator Blunt, who, in the past, had warmly received me into his Capitol Hill office, would not reply to my question, which is answer enough, isn't it?

There is a very sad history in our country of revolving door deals in which elected officials and highly placed government employees leave their public offices to be handsomely rewarded for their loyalty to special interests and government contract recipients with high paying jobs and lobbyist positions. I believe that it would be helpful for all elected officials to be barred from even the appearance of unethical, back room deals by nailing shut Washington's revolving door system.

Rhetoric and Reality

> When a candidate promises what clearly cannot be done, such as Governor Mike Huckabee's suggestion that he would consider using military force to stop abortions or Donald Trump's promise to make Mexico pay for erecting a fence between our nations, why would anyone continue to support his or her candidacy?

> While any candidate might be excessively hopeful or even simply mistaken, shouldn't it be illegal to be intentionally deceptive in campaign promises?

> Why is it that Presidents avoid criminal prosecution for things like selling weapons to Iran, arming rebels illegally in Nicaragua, or lying about WMDs to start a war?

He wasn't specifically talking about politics when Yoda said to Luke Skywalker, "Difficult to see. Always in motion is the future." And yet it is good advice for those of us who write about politics

As a young graduate student, I predicted that Ronald Reagan had no chance of winning election because no one would fall for his obviously self-contradictory promises of lowering taxes, increasing military spending, and balancing the budget. No one who could pass first grade math would believe in the "supply side" economics that his own budget director, David Stockman, had called a "Trojan horse" for the poor. Yet Reagan not only won in 1980, but even after the total failure of supply side economics, resulting in record setting deficit spending, he was re-elected in 1984 and is still referenced as a conservative hero.

I was confident that the public would never fall for George W. Bush's claim that there were weapons of mass destruction hidden in Iraq. Two hundred weapons inspectors had failed to find any evidence of such weapons, and their director, Scott Ritter, was pleading with Bush not to start a war on grounds that had been thoroughly refuted by existing intelligence. Once Bush's illegal war had been irrecoverably started, I predicted that Bush would be removed from office and put on trial for war crimes. Instead, he was elected to a second term and is now writing memoirs from retirement, still trying to plaster the dung wall of his lethal and economically disastrous decisions.

I have stopped making predictions based on confidence in voter logic. If I could recapture any of my earlier naïveté about the original motivations of the Tea Party, I would probably be writing about how the Tea Party would likely rebel against its former candidates. Their newly elected class of legislators started its tenure by borrowing $36 billion from China to continue the Bush era tax cuts for the super-rich. The Tea Party was driven by language of cutting the deficit, stopping runaway spending, and a cessation of borrowing from foreign countries. But voter memory is very short and its capacity for forgiving hypocrisy is limitless.

All of the critics of the anticipated deficits created by Obama's health-care reform were silent about the much larger deficit created by Bush's tax cut for the wealthy. When put to the test, there was not a modicum of sincerity to all of the language about deficit spending. The real agenda was to do what the Republican Party always seems to be intent upon, giving tax breaks to the wealthy and saddling the poor with spiraling national debt.

When will the middle class grow weary of this exercise of buying bullets for its own assassins?

What's The Matter with America?

Thomas Frank's 2005 book, *What's the Matter with Kansas?*, sought to chronicle the degeneration of a progressive state into a state in which the poor and the middle class consistently vote against their own interests. Though the whole of the United States does not have a progressive history, it does seem that in most states, voters have been conditioned by the rhetoric of fear and moral judgment to vote against their own economic interests. Is there a way to educate voters to be better at critically evaluating their choices?

Since there is both a fierce religious and social resistance in Middle Eastern Muslim states to having foreign and non-Islamic armies

on their soil, can the United States reasonably be expected to invade any country in that region and be greeted as liberators?

If you had been aware that your personal tax burden for the costs of invading Iraq would amount to more than $10,000 would you have supported the invasion?

After costly legislative mistakes, both the federal government and most state governments now require that an economic impact statement be attached to any piece of legislation under consideration. There are lots of good ideas in the world that simply cost too much to be seriously considered.

It is too bad that we could not require the same sort of economic impact statement in foreign policy decisions. In 2003, we were told that the American people would not have to pay anything for the invasion of Iraq. The Bush administration assured its critics that oil proceeds from the vast resources of Iraq would pay for the invasion, we would be welcomed as liberators, and we would be able to destroy Iraq's stockpile of weapons of mass destruction. Of course, in my columns during that time period I was pointing out the fact that this was just Soviet-styled propaganda. Weapons inspectors had already reported that there were no weapons of mass destruction in Iraq. Those who had spent as much as a couple of hours exposing themselves to Muslim thought and religion would have known that we would not be greeted as liberators, and of course, the economic impact estimate was an outrageous lie.

Within a few months the Bush administration had recalculated and offered the public the figure of $80 billion, a shockingly high number. I and others waxed poetic about what we could have done for poverty, education, and health issues in the United States with that same sum of money, but of course, the estimate was just another Republican attempt at public deception. The real figure was not $80 billion nor was it $800 billion. The best estimate is that our decision to invade Iraq will cost Americans $2.4 trillion, thirty times the 2003 propaganda.

In a column at that time, I asked readers, "Would you favor the invasion of Iraq if you knew that the real implication is that you would have to delay your retirement and continue to work for three or four more years to pay for this war?" Ironically, my estimate was too low. The House Minority Leader at the time, Ohio Republican congressman John Boehner, suggested that the Social Security retirement age be raised to 70 in order to pay for the wars in Iraq and Afghanistan. Are you sufficiently pleased with the outcomes of our wars that you are gladly willing to work five years longer to pay for them?

Of course, people who are wealthy won't have to work those extra years, just the 53 million Americans who are dependent on Social Security. Rep. Boehner has demonstrated that the "grand old party" has become an exclusive club of billionaires squeezing the life out of middle class Americans.

And yet, the midterm elections in Obama's first term put Republicans back in the majority of Congress. Are our memories really so short, or have we accepted rule by the aristocracy? It seems self-evident to me that voting for a Republican is like buying a lottery ticket. The lottery serves the interests of a very few people at the expense of millions of gullible ticket buyers who hope against hope (or who are being punished for not paying attention in math class) that they will become one of the rich few.

3

Military

"...fighting for peace is like copulating for virginity," (a publishable approximation of George Carlin's observation)

Missing the Point in Afghanistan

The three most famous "leakers" or "whistle blowers," Chelsea Manning, Julian Assange, and Edward Snowden, certainly revealed a lot to the American people about both domestic spying and our military adventures abroad. Did they do the American public a favor or are they deserving of condemnation for treason?

If you had taken a vow to keep confidential government documents secret but you became aware of treasonous actions by government officials, are you obligated to keep the government secrets or do you owe a debt to society to alert the public of the misdeeds?

Do military officers sacrifice the right to free speech so that their loyalty to the President in the role of commander-in-chief is kept sacred or can a citizen army remain intact with officers maintaining an individual right to express their views?

When General Stanley McChrystal made critical remarks about President Obama in the midst of an interview given to *Rolling Stone*, the news media buzz was all about the inevitable dismissal of General McChrystal and the popular decision to ask General David Petraeus to take over the effort in Afghanistan. What was missing from the public furor was any discussion of what McChrystal had actually said about the war in Afghanistan. Following the release of more than 90,000 field reports by WikiLeaks (the online leak reporting service withheld about 15,000 reports that it considered to have information that might have endangered troops on the ground) the conversation in the media again missed the point and focused on trying to figure out who leaked the information. Clearly, whoever the source is, that person is in "deep kimchi," but the real story was largely ignored.

We, the citizens fielding this foreign occupation force that was ostensibly fighting on our behalf, need to deal with the issues that this rogue source turned over to WikiLeaks and what prompted General McChrystal to become so disillusioned with the war and his commander-in-chief. We spent more than a decade fighting in Afghanistan (World War II, by comparison, lasted for six years) and have little to show for the sacrifices involved. The war became increasingly lethal, expensive, and apparently unwinnable. The case for war in Afghanistan was always very thin. The prospects of a meaningful victory were ephemeral, and in the end, unrealized.

Our real enemies, so far as the threat of terrorism is concerned, reside in countries that are either so divided for and against us, i.e., Pakistan, or so economically entangled with us, i.e., Saudi Arabia, that we cannot use the blunt force of military invasion where it might actually make sense.

Regardless of what you may think of "leakers" like Chelsea Manning, Julian Assange, and Edward Snowden, what we cannot deny is that the Obama administration, which we elected on a sea of sentiment for change, was hiding the facts and feeding the public propaganda in much the same way as the former administration.

Even the much-heralded discovery of vast mineral wealth in the mountains of Afghanistan has been shown to be a hoax. The "discovery" was "leaked" to give American taxpayers some hope of relief from the financial obligation of caring for this country that we have spoiled. The sad truth is that the "recent discovery" was found in Russian geological surveys from thirty years ago.

While conservative pundits call Obama a socialist and worse, the truth appears that he may be just a more articulate version of previous, dishonest right-wing office holders. We can only hope that there have been important lessons learned from this failed experiment in nation building.

Occupation of Foreign Nations in the Twenty-First Century

The colonial empires of Britain, Spain, France, and Holland have given way to the less evident economic colonialism of the United States, China, and their rivals. As we move into the future, can you envision a world marketplace that allows for trade that creates wealth on both sides of a transaction, leaving both nations with more sovereignty?

If China invaded and occupied the United States and under their administration America were to reach full employment, have universal healthcare, a rebuilt infrastructure and a shift to sustainable energy sources, could you see the Chinese occupation of America as a good thing?

Should the American government take measures to prevent our powerful corporations from making political contributions to campaigns in the foreign nations where we influence governments for favorable treatment of our energy, agriculture, and labor markets?

The irreverent Monty Python movie, *Life of Brian*, parodies the religious and political mix of first-century Palestine. Its iconoclastic snipes at the Christian gospels aside, there is one noteworthy scene in which John Cleese's character, a Jewish Zealot, repeatedly asks "What have the Romans ever done for us?" The frank answers from his fellow Zealots seemed to undermine their insurgent enthusiasm, because the Romans had brought roads, commerce, clean water, and sewers.

The historical fact is that the Romans eventually turned to a "final solution" in Palestine, attempting to kill every Jew they could find because the Jews were impossible to rule. Like modern Iraqis and Afghanis, the Jews didn't want to be ruled, even if the occupying forces offered them a better standard of living.

One can imagine a group of modern zealous insurgents in Afghanistan asking one another, "What has America ever done for us?" Our stated goals for keeping more than 60,000 American soldiers in Afghanistan all sounded like we should be heroes among the Afghanis. However, we were treated to years of daily news reports of violent resistance to our attempts at establishing a democratic government, decent healthcare, and education for both boys and girls, and an economy based on something other than growing poppies for the opium trade. We wanted to create an economically viable, democratic Afghanistan but the question that should plague the American voter is whether that noble goal can be accomplished through a military occupation?

Unlike most of the contributors to local newspaper opinion pages, I am inclined to believe that President Obama is an intelligent, trustworthy, and well-intentioned commander in chief. I wanted to trust the President; however, I find myself to be cavalier about our modern occupation of foreign lands, not just as Afghanistan has lived up to its reputation as the "graveyard of empires," but in the more general awareness that nineteenth century colonialism and twentieth century economic colonialism will not work in the twenty-first century.

It's All about Whose Ox is Being Gored

> What right do nations who have nuclear weapons have to prevent other nations from acquiring the same? We don't want Iran to get the bomb but many of its neighbors already have nuclear weapons. Movies that cast aspersions on the government of North Korea are not accurate and yet not entirely based on fantasy. The current nuclear club has shown restraint but does that equate to reliable virtue?

> Is there any fail-safe way to make the earth a nuclear free zone?

> Nuclear power plants do not equate to weapons grade uranium but they do provide a lot of the material necessary for extremely lethal dirty bombs. Can we rely on cheap electricity from nuclear power plants when we are creating hard to store and ever harder to secure dirty bomb materials?

When my father said, "I don't know why we are still sending our soldiers to fight in Afghanistan when we've got perfectly good nuclear bombs we haven't even used yet!" the foreign policy discussion at his 90th birthday party ended. He was old then, but regrettably, this wasn't something he would not have said fifty years earlier.

He fought in the South Pacific during WWII and his horrible experiences landed him in a mental hospital at the end of the war with what was called "battle fatigue," now known as Post-Traumatic Stress Disorder. In his mind, the terror of warfare is so horrible that no one he cares about should ever be subjected to it. Sadly, however, the only people he cared about are American soldiers. To him, killing every man, woman, and child in Afghanistan would be acceptable if we could avoid the loss of a single American life.

I don't fault my father for not being very objective about this. Everyone he went through basic training with, everyone who mattered to him in a personal way, died in combat during WWII. Many people who live in Israel, Palestine, Iraq, or Iran have similar feelings. They have lost so many family and friends that the lives of "others" have little or no value.

And therein lies the difficulty in our present dilemma of nuclear proliferation. We don't want Iran, North Korea, or any hostile nation to have nuclear weapons, because we are afraid that they would use them. They want them because they know that we have lots of nuclear weapons and we are never more than one election away from using our arsenal. Thankfully, my father never ran for public office, but a lot of the people who will be running in future elections are not far from his view of international affairs.

After all, you cannot find out how many Iraqi or Afghani casualties there were during our recent Middle Eastern wars because, as the Bush administration once explained, we don't keep count of enemy casualties. We count our own. We count our money. We count our equipment. But we don't count what doesn't matter to us and that includes the lives of the poor peasants who have been sent to die in front of our armies.

It would only take about fifty pounds of weapons grade uranium to produce a bomb that could wipe out any city in the world. Given that there are now more than a thousand tons of weapons grade uranium in the world, much of it in the questionable management of unstable governments, it is reasonable to assume that the greatest challenge to world security still comes from the threat of nuclear bombs.

We have not always done a very good job of keeping up with where we have stored our own nuclear bombs. It would be impossible to accurately keep up with the entire world's supply. Our only real hope of avoiding a nuclear nightmare is to tone down the rhetoric and do the things that make for international peace.

Curbing Military Spending

Are you willing to pay for military hardware that will never be used? If not, how can you avoid it?

President Eisenhower's famous warnings against the power of the military industrial complex are very familiar to us, and yet, we appear to have done nothing in light of those warnings to curb their lobbying power. What can we do now?

Are you concerned about the "brain drain" taken up by the military industrial complex (beyond all of the capital resources it siphons off of our nation)?

If you receive a bill for $5000 for something you didn't order, and you don't want, and wouldn't use if you had it, would you pay the bill? No? Oh yes you will. You will pay it because it will come to you in the form of federal taxes to pay more than $6,000,000,000 for twenty-five C-17 military cargo planes that the military does not want and cannot possibly use. Don't worry though, when we discover that we don't have crews to fly them or places to store them we'll do with them what we did with the last batch of C-17s we didn't need. Did you know that we sold these planes to several Arab countries so that they can move their troops into place to fight our troops the next time we expand our wars in the Middle East? Where is Rush Limbaugh when you need him?

On April 6, 2009, the Secretary of Defense, Robert Gates, announced that we would not be ordering any more C-17s, but he was too new on the job to understand that such decisions are not actually made by the elected government of the United States. Boeing currently has much more power over the way federal tax dollars are spent than does the American President, and after Gates said "No more!" the Congress placed an order for eight more in May and seventeen more in June. And you get to write the checks.

We could end this kind of corporate control of government if we could ever pass meaningful campaign finance reform. However, there is no chance of that happening in the foreseeable future. With the Supreme Court putting democracy on the block for sale to the highest bidder.

The only realistic measure that might bring this kind of runaway spending to a halt would be to give the president some real budget power by granting a line item veto. Most governors have line item vetoes to keep state budgets balanced.

Part of what made it possible for Bill Clinton to balance the federal budget is because congress briefly gave him a line item veto in 1996, but by 1998 our friends on the Supreme Court ruled that it was unconstitutional. This would not have happened if the line item veto authority were being exercised by a Republican, but the die has now been cast, and only an amendment to the constitution can restore this authority to the president.

Of course, the line item veto would not be so crucial if legislators would just refrain from attaching pork amendments to bills. Some legislators, including Missouri's Senator Claire McCaskill, have refused to use "ear marks" to send pork barrel projects back to the states. As much as I admire McCaskill's principled stand on this issue, it really ends up hurting Missouri if other senators are not compelled to do the same because tax dollars from my adopted state are funding pork in other states. I wonder, however, if Boeing would allow us to amend the constitution, realizing that it would give actual power to the President?

Wars That End With a Whimper

> It seems clear that the United States invaded Iraq on false pretenses, and though we did remove a cruel dictator from power, we seem to have left the country less stable and more violent. Can an occupation force fix a nation that doesn't want a foreign fix?

> If Iraq as a sovereign nation really no longer exists, does the United States have a military role to play in establishing new boundaries for a divided nation?

> It appears that by destroying the integrity of Iraq as a military balance to Iran, we may have basically strengthened Iran's role in the region. Does the United States have a military role to play in containing Iranian influence in Syria, Iraq, and other struggling nations in the Middle East?

The war in Iraq ended without tickertape parades and without sending much of a ripple across the world's media. After eight years of war, more than a trillion dollars of unfunded military spending, and more importantly, the loss of 4500 American soldiers' lives, ten times that many injured, and tens of thousands of Iraqi civilian deaths, the war ended with no real sense of accomplishment. There was not much celebration because we just don't know how to feel about it. The same was true of the "final" withdrawal from Afghanistan.

Those of us who stood on public street corners holding signs and singing songs in protest of the invasion of Iraq in 2003 have not gathered to hold signs saying, "See, we told you so." One of my articles from that time said something like, "fighting for peace is like copulating for virginity," (a *publishable approximation of George Carlin's observation)*—it just doesn't work that way. And there is no joy in having been right about this blood bath.

Dick Cheney and his daughter, Elizabeth, continue trying to build a case for an invasion of Iran, but I hope that the American public has lost its taste for pre-emptive war. I am cynical enough to believe that Cheney's motivation now is not much different from his motivation in pushing the Iraq war on President Bush: the transfer of wealth into the hands of the military industrial corporations where he and his peers have all gotten nasty rich. The loss of lives in war just doesn't seem to bother him the way it would a normal human being. I'm a pastor, so I am not supposed to hate anyone, but I believe that I love Dick Cheney less than anyone else on earth.

In the past years we have seen the people's will to be free express itself through both the Arab Spring in the Middle East and the Occupy movement in America and Europe. I hope we have learned that while we may support and assist a revolution, we cannot export democracy the way we still send Coca-Cola and American cigarettes around the world. It remains to be seen if the governments emerging from the Arab revolutions will become friends of the United States, but I am inclined to think that our friendships with the governments of Iraq and Afghanistan, after our occupation fades in memory, will be more window dressing than true love.

In the twenty-first century, traditional warfare will not accomplish the goals for which we went to war in the first half of the twentieth. The good news is that we have more effective tools for achieving stability and world peace through science and economic policy. Alternative energy sources offer a potential end to dependence on foreign oil. Cell phones and the Internet undermine the isolation and propaganda used by oppressive governments (including our own) to control the collective consciousness. As we welcome home our remaining combat forces from our last wars of adventurism, let us resolve never to be quietly led down the path to another unnecessary conflict.

Yes, We Do Torture Prisoners

> Since the fact is clearly documented that American military personnel tortured prisoners by order of the Bush administration, why have there been no charges brought for war crimes?

> Are there circumstances, either on the battlefield or in stopping a potential terrorist act, that would justify torturing a prisoner?

Does our recent history of torturing prisoners of war increase the chances that our own captured soldiers might be tortured?

Geneva Conventions have been treated as if there were antiquated or mere suggestions. How might we actually enforce these long standing values regarding the just treatment of prisoners?

On my first visit to the Tower of London, I was intrigued by the display of cruel torture devices on display there that had been used on seventeenth century prisoners. A few years later when I took my daughter to visit London, we were surprised to learn that the display had been removed, and the staff no longer wanted to discuss any part of England's history of horrible torture.

Denial doesn't change history, but it seems to be a natural reflex. No nation wants to own its lapses in moral decision-making, though both Japan and Germany made progress as nations once they had acknowledged their perpetration of atrocities in war. Americans, however, have a legendary resistance to self-criticism.

Top-secret documents of the CIA and the Justice Department have been declassified as a direct result of a lawsuit filed by the ACLU. These memos related to interrogation techniques used in the "war on terrorism" document the official US position on aggressive interrogation/torture from 2002 to 2008. The four memos, taken together, are about 400 pages of very specific instructions about how to slap a prisoner to insult without injuring and how long a person can be kept in a box with insects; suggestions are even given of non-stinging insects to use.

The documents attempt to make even water boarding sound like a humane interrogation technique, because even though it makes the subject feel like he or she is drowning, actual death is unlikely. The allegation that the United States had made top-level decisions to ignore the Geneva Convention standards regarding torture has drawn a collective yawn from most of the American public.

We are desensitized by having watched the fictitious interrogations in "ticking bomb" scenarios in such popular TV shows as "24 Hours" and "Law and Order." That President Bush had authorized torture has been little more than a subtext in the media with only a few civil liberties and religious groups attempting to challenge these practices.

On the practical level, even interrogators have discussed the unreliability of information gained through torture, as anyone threatened with drowning on a water board will say almost anything to make the torture stop. The best information appears to have been gained over a seemingly casual dinner and a cup of coffee. However, the fact that we decided, at our highest government levels, to use torture is a moral travesty. The indifference of the American people is horrifying.

Though soldiers who used water boarding in the Vietnam War were prosecuted, it makes no sense to go after military personnel in this case, because their actions were authorized by our former President. However, morally, we all need to wake up and make it clear that we will never again accept a dismissal of our conscience in the service of our fear. Criminal prosecution of our former president may be a necessary part of making this point.

Exploitation of Vulnerable Nations

Since our federal policies have a huge impact on the security and economies of other nations, should those nations be allowed to influence our elections through political donations, campaigning, or threats of military action?

If, in fact, the US government has attempted to influence the outcome of foreign elections through political donations, campaigning, and threats of military action, should we take measures to make certain that we don't engage in this kind of military/political colonialism in the future?

If an Arab country chooses to elect a religiously radical government, or if a Central American country chooses to elect a communist or socialist government, do we have a right to intervene?

President Obama assured us in a policy speech on Afghanistan that the United States does not invade countries to control their territory or to exploit their natural resources, but it is clear that this claim is not historically true (I suspect that it is not even currently true). In a 1962 testimony before the United States Senate, the Secretary of State, Dean Rusk, listed more than one hundred instances of Americans using military force to intervene in the actions of foreign governments, in order to persuade the Senate to use our military against Cuba's growing bond with the Soviet Union.

I am personally familiar with the case of Nicaragua, which we invaded in 1853 and again in 1854 and then again in 1894. After that, we put the Samosa family into power and operated the Nicaraguan government through this family of bloody dictators. I have stood on the crater ridge of the Masaya Volcano outside of Managua, now a national park, which was a favorite spot where the Samosas had their political opponents dropped from American military helicopters into the pit of the active volcano. The screams of the activist priests and politicians falling to their violent deaths sent a message to the Nicaraguans that they could not resist the American control of their nation.

And yet they did resist, and in the 1980s, the Sandinistas took power and the armies of the Samosa dictators fled into neighboring countries. President Reagan wanted to supply the Samosa military and send them back in to regain control of Nicaragua, but Congress wouldn't go along with it, making it illegal to send support to the cruel dictator's forces. Reagan re-named Samosa's army the "Contras" and called them "Freedom Fighters," which has to go down as one of the biggest lies ever sold to the American people.

In spite of the unconstitutional, and morally reprehensible nature of it, the Reagan administration, through its henchman, Oliver North, actually sold weapons to known terrorists in Iran to raise money to provide weapons to our own terrorists in Nicaragua. This outrageous act makes it impossible for me to believe that Reagan retired and when on to earn millions of dollars on the speaking network, rather than go straight to prison for treason.

As recently as 2006, when Daniel Ortega was again running for president of Nicaragua, President George W. Bush called Colonel Ollie North out of retirement and sent this leader of a terrorist war against the poor of Nicaragua back to Managua to campaign against Ortega. Can you imagine how we would react if Osama Bin Laden had come to the US to campaign against one of our presidential candidates in 2008? That is how it felt to the people of Nicaragua—America once again threatening to use state sponsored terrorism to control their nation. Predictably, Ortega was elected, which should be a lesson to future administrations about what doesn't work in foreign policy.

Ratcheting up the war against Afghanistan is exactly what we have done wrong for more than a century. The industries that supply our military are driving our foreign policy, thereby creating new generations of terrorists. The reason we do not see Nicaraguan terrorists on our borders is because most of what Nicaraguans see and experience of Americans is from the Non-Governmental Organizations that provide food, medicine, education, and housing for their poor. American charities have helped to heal Central Americans' hostility towards us such that you and I can feel safe walking through the streets of Matagalpa, where the bullet-pocked walls still cry out in protest of a different time when we were the terrorists and they were the victims.

So, Mr. President, though I am saddened that you have succumbed to the Washington pressure to do everything in the most expensive, violent, and ineffective manner possible, when you are ready to really change the way our government works, let's lay down the guns and send teachers, doctors, agricultural specialists, and small business incentives to Afghanistan, and we'll finally begin to win the war on terrorism. You know that I'm right, even though people like me don't have lobbyists in Washington, DC pulling the purse strings.

Will the Real Traitor Please Stand Up?

From Russia, where he has been granted asylum, Edward Snowden, accused of being a traitor, asked, "If I am a traitor, who did I betray? I gave all of my information to the American public, to American journalists." Granted, that's not technically a good legal defense, but morally, do you agree?

After Chelsea (formerly Bradley) Manning's ardent attempts to go through the proper military channels to have the war crimes he knew about addressed, was he justified in taking the evidence to the press?

In light of the more than 30,000 annual gun deaths in America, why is the National Rifle Association not widely viewed as supporting domestic terrorism?

I maintain hope that we will avoid lethal military involvement in Syria, even if it is predicated on what amounted to a blunder on the part of Secretary of State Kerry, whose accidentally offered diplomatic solution was accepted and it actually resulted in the removal of chemical weapons from the Syrian battlefield.

Still, President Obama presented a passionate and sadly hypocritical case for launching approximately $100 million in ordinance at military sites in Syria while insisting that it would not be starting a war. Really, Mr. President? If Canada launched one hundred missiles at military sites in the United States, would we consider that an act of war?

Our President has asked us to watch the videos of children dying from exposure to chemical weapons in Syria, but let's be honest—this administration arrested Bradley (now "Chelsea") Manning and tortured this 22-year-old soldier for a year before putting him on trial. Manning had viewed video of American war crimes, in which our forces had fired on unarmed journalists and civilians, then fired again at first responders, killing children in the process, and even desecrated the bodies by driving over them until the bodies broke into pieces, while American observers joked about what they were doing. Manning reported the evidence to superiors who, in violation of military law, ignored him. He then leaked the material to the public, and turned himself in to face trial.

The soldiers who committed these heinous crimes were never charged, nor even reprimanded. Manning will be in prison for three decades. If our President were actually concerned about war crimes in which children are killed, wouldn't we first be concerned about when we do it rather than putting the whistle blowers in solitary confinement for decades? If we are concerned about the horrors of killing civilians, wouldn't we stop our own drone strikes in foreign lands where our flying robots have killed thousands of children, women, and farmers?

If we are concerned about chemical weapons, and we certainly should be, wouldn't our first measure be to destroy our own arsenal of nuclear weapons of mass destruction that are many times more dangerous than Syria's chemical weapons? And shouldn't we be concerned about the chemical weapons stockpiled with American subsidies in Egypt and Israel?

Every news source other than our government places the chemical weapon death toll in Syria at less than half of what the Obama administration has trumpeted, but even if you take the president's numbers as being accurate, more than twice as many Americans die at the hands of domestic gun owners every month as were killed in the incident in Syria. We know that the government's failure to stem the 30,000 annual gun deaths in America is due to nothing more than the political donations made by gun manufacturers. If we are willing to turn a blind eye to domestic violence (and really, isn't this terrorism of the worst sort?) resulting in tens of thousands of entirely preventable deaths every year because of political donations, then where do we find the moral authority to tell Syria that its conduct is immoral? It is certainly no more immoral than our own!

If we want to save lives from being lost in a lethal civil war, we could save many more by launching those missiles at our own gun manufacturing industry. At the very least, President Obama should return his Nobel Peace Prize. He doesn't deserve it.

If All You have is a Hammer the Whole World Looks like a Nail

> It is impossible and, frankly a horrifying proposition, to put a dollar value on human life. Looking purely at the economic cost of the wars in which we have been engaged in the past fifty years, in your opinion, which ones had results that justified the expenditure?
>
> Had we left Saddam Hussein in power in Iraq, would living conditions be better there for the average citizen?
>
> Budget money transferred to battlefield expenditures come at the expense of domestic infrastructure spending. Has it been worth it?

Twenty years ago, Sting recorded the belief that he had never seen a military solution that didn't end up as something worse, in his song, *"If I Ever Lose My Faith in You."* I can think of what I believe to have been historical exceptions to that poetic statement, and yet it seems to be generally true. As bad as Saddam Hussein was, he didn't kill as many civilians as we did in the process of "liberating" Iraq. As bad as the Taliban were in Afghanistan, the expenditure of twelve years of American life and wealth does not appear to have made a permanent change in the character of that nation.

Consider what impact it would have had on our economy, on our shrinking middle class, on our growing income gap in America if, rather than invading Afghanistan and Iraq we had made colleges and universities tuition-free for Americans for the next twenty-five years. Making higher education free would have dramatically changed the future for a generation, and would have cost significantly less than our last two ill-advised wars.

Given a choice between better roads, bridges, dams and a modernized power grid or invading another Middle Eastern nation, not many people would say, "I want Saddam removed from power even if it means that one of my kids has to die on the battlefield, the other three can't go to college, and I will become unemployed and homeless." Though that is exactly what happens. After all the bodies are buried, stockholders in the machinery of war are much wealthier and the people of Iraq are not much better off.

Kids who want to go to college don't have a lobbyist. Military manufacturers do. And even though the construction industry does have lobbyists, it does not have the same clout in political donations that the military industrial complex has. Spending on military action is much more profitable than building schools, roads, bridges, and dams, but creates far fewer jobs.[1]

I believe that there are times when we can use our military to achieve honorable and moral goals, but neither honor nor morality have figured heavily in decision-making in recent years; only profit has. Our power grid is antiquated. Our bridges are crumbling. Our levees are leaking. The poor are becoming locked into permanent poverty, and higher education is increasingly out of reach. Before any of us sign off on another military course of action, we should look around us and see what we are willing to personally sacrifice to achieve the stated goal. If the goal doesn't justify the cost, then maybe we need to keep our bombs and missiles to ourselves.

1. Pollen and Garrett-Peltier, "The U.S. Employment Effects of Military and Domestic Spending Priorities: An Updated Analysis."

SECTION II

Economic

4

Poverty and Education

According to Gandhi, "Poverty is the worst form of violence."

When Howard Zinn Died

While facts are neither conservative nor liberal, how you report the facts always comes with a certain amount of spin. Given that public school textbooks must be fairly brief, how do we arrive at a fair and honest way of talking about our own history that is as free as possible of manipulative misinformation?

The westward growth of the United States involved both displacement of, and wars with, indigenous Indians and land theft from Mexico. Is it unpatriotic to be honest about those chapters of American history?

The evolution of labor practices in the United States is rarely discussed beyond the end of slavery in the Civil War. How informed do you feel that you are on the role of labor unions and the progress of worker safety and employment security laws?

When Steve Jobs gave the world the iPad (yawn) and President Obama delivered his first State of the Union address (zzz . . .) the headline of the day, at least for those of us who long to know what is really going on in the world, was the death of Howard Zinn. The media consistently insisted on calling Zinn a "radical" or a "leftist," but as I have reflected on his life and career, I do not find him to be either radical or leftist. He was one of the few public figures in America who told the unvarnished truth.

I left a study group that was discussing Howard Zinn's most influential book, *A People's History of the United States*, to join friends in a State of the Union watch party. That transition was like falling through Alice's "Looking Glass." Zinn's career as a historian has pierced the veil of propaganda to reveal the truth behind an array of subjects: the European settlement of this continent, our institution of slavery, our wars against the American Indians, our theft of land from Mexico, our trumped up reasons for going to war in many instances, our repression of labor unions, our resistance to the Civil Rights movement, and many things about modern wars from Vietnam to Iraq about which the news media always seems to be silent.

The State of the Union address reiterated tired old campaign speeches . . . Hey, wasn't the vow to stop giving tax breaks to corporations who export jobs Ross Perot's idea? Frankly, I expected President Bush to lie to the public and he never disappointed me. When President Obama adamantly announced that all combat troops would be out of Iraq by the end of August of 2009, you have to know how to dissect political doublespeak to know what he is saying and what he is not saying. All "combat" troops would be out by the end of August but the POTUS always planned to still have 50,000 Americans in uniform in Iraq, and to continue to spend billions of dollars on Iraq that we borrow from China, because no matter whom we elect to be president, our nation is apparently now run by the corporations who get our tax dollars. The eventual removal of American troops from Iraq was not to satisfy a promise made by President Obama. It was due to a lack of cooperation on the part of the newly installed government of Iraq. Bush seemed to have an empty head, and Obama, it seems to me, is an empty suit.

I had the good fortune of hearing Howard Zinn lecture three times in one year: twice in Missouri universities, and finally at Harvard. In each setting you could see students reacting as if electricity was running through the room. Some were shocked; many were angry because they were hearing things which, if they were true, could only mean that they had been lied to by teachers and text books for most of their lives. Reading his books is a painful exercise, because popular myths are torn down in the face of historical facts. Ironically, because he was willing to tell the truth about historical events, his work has been marginalized by being labeled as "liberal," because we are a nation that would rather cling to a comfortable lie than to accept an inconvenient truth.

When I was a child, the media enjoyed making fun of gullible Russians who fell for their government's outrageous propaganda. Now, it seems, we have become the brunt of our own jokes.

Illiteracy in America

Illiteracy in America is estimated to be static over the past decade at 14 percent of our population, far worse than in some developing countries. Could you navigate life in America without being able to read?

Literacy is a relative target. While 14 percent are believed to be simply unable to read, 21 percent read below the fifth grade level. Would you hire an employee who couldn't read above the fifth grade level?[1]

Being unable to read in our society leads not only to poverty, but since 70 percent of prisoners read below the fourth grade level, we cannot realistically deny the connection between crime and illiteracy. Can we require prisons to set literacy as a goal to be reached before parole?

In Charles Dickens' "A Christmas Carol" (still the best Christmas sermon ever written) Scrooge notices claw-like protrusions under the robe of the Ghost of Christmas Present. The spirit pulls his robe open to reveal two starving children. Scrooge asks, "Whose are they?" and with moral precision, the spirit shouts, "They are yours!" He explains, "This boy is Ignorance. This girl is Want. Beware them both but most of all beware this boy, for on his brow I see that written which is Doom." Dickens was right on target. Poverty is a horrible form of violence, but ignorance in the form of illiteracy and incompetence in math spells doom for the individual and for our society.

A lot of us in helping professions focus on meeting immediate needs, giving food to the hungry and shelter to the homeless, but the ultimate solution to poverty never comes from just scratching where it itches. Poverty is a very complicated problem and the effective solutions to it are no less complex. And yet, no single cure for poverty is as important as education. Literacy and a high school diploma are crucial to escaping the gravitational pull that keeps people in hopeless poverty.

1. Huffington Post, "The U.S. Illiteracy Rate Hasn't Changed In 10 Years."

With a growing number of adults realizing that their only chance of becoming self-supporting is to take the time to gain the literacy skills they did not acquire in their childhood school experiences, there is a never-ending need for volunteers to help share the gift of reading. Literacy is a gift most of us can afford to give since it is given as a gift of time. All of us who work in the nonprofit world depend upon the cash donations from our supporters but every bit as important as our financial supporters are the volunteers who have the time and compassion to give of themselves to those who are in need.

A college student or a retiree who is barely getting by and cannot make cash donations can still change the destiny of another person's life by giving some time for one-on-one tutoring. It is no exaggeration to estimate the lifetime wage difference for a twenty-five year old who earns her or his GED may be more than $20,000 a year, amounting to as much as a million dollars over a working career. With that increased income comes more stable families, a lower crime rate, and a general relief of suffering in our society. Helping an adult student to gain math and literacy skills is one of those "ripple effect" opportunities in which anyone with some spare time can change the world, one person at a time.

In the city where I live, we typically have more than thirty young adults, many of whom are among the homeless population, who are in need of tutors. A local community college operates a GED training program that is helping many of these young people and yet, not everyone is ready for GED training. Many will need remedial help before even starting to work on a GED. There is a literacy program in almost every city with people in need waiting for those who are willing to give them some time and attention. Or, you could watch some more daytime TV.

Poverty is Unnecessary Violence

When there are not enough jobs and there is not enough public housing and charities don't pick up the slack, what happens to a homeless person?

Does the government have an obligation to keep people alive that have failed in school and at work, who have alienated their family members and who, perhaps, also have a criminal record? Is it okay to let them die from exposure?

Many western European countries appear to have solved the problem of chronic homelessness. Would their solutions work in the United States?

According to Mahatma Gandhi, "Poverty is the worst form of violence." This has seemed to me to be especially true on the nights when the temperature goes far below freezing. Everyone who is homeless does not live in a homeless shelter. The shelters are often filled to capacity and they are always overfilled when it is freezing outside. There are people who are not allowed in the shelters, and sometimes the reasons can seem pretty cruel, but the people who run shelters have rules and I can't fault them for trying to keep the shelters safe and peaceful.

I spend time every week with the people who live on the streets. Some sleep in their cars, others find sewers, drain pipes, or bridges to call home. Others, like "Tim" live in a tent hidden in woods on someone's property, trying to avoid detection. Every year I try to collect tents, sleeping bags, coats, gloves and blankets to give to people like Tim. There is never enough and most camping gear doesn't stand up to daily use, month after month.

On terribly cold nights, Tim burns candles in a coffee can inside of his tent. He has to try to shield some of the light of the candles with tin foil to avoid giving away his location (another local resident set his tent on fire while he slept using the same heating method . . . he did not survive). Tim looks a bit out of place standing in line to eat with the other homeless women and men who gather in the warming station where my friends and I serve lunch once a week. His military style haircut and strong frame could easily lead you to assume that he is a soldier or a law enforcement officer, but he is not.

Tim works temporary jobs when he can, and has traveled from state to state over the past few years wherever he could find a job that would last for a few weeks or months. Manual labor jobs in construction or shipping are often quite brief, so he is experienced in finding his way through homeless shelters and poverty programs, but when he finds work he works. When he can't, he volunteers to help people like me who are trying to provide survival gear and food to the unsheltered homeless.

He readily expresses gratitude for the gift of a tent and sleeping bag, for his coat and gloves, and when he eats with the church groups who bring meals, he is always very complimentary. Still, I would argue, that he is a victim of violence.

There is no one person or institution to blame for this violence but the point is that poverty results in cruelty to humans that should be intolerable to our society. No one will leave his or her dog or cat outside in sub-zero weather, but Tim will go back to the tent where he has lived for the last few months and try to stay warm with a candle in a coffee can on those nights. If it were just Tim, or even just a dozen people like Tim, this essay wouldn't find its way into print, but the homeless who have run out of welcome in the shelters number in the thousands across our land.

Last week, in the line of people waiting for a hot lunch was a young woman with a six-week-old baby and an elderly gentleman on a cane who had recently suffered a stroke. You didn't see any of these people on TV in the gallery when the President delivered his last State of the Union Address but this is, in fact, the real state of our nation where there are not enough jobs, affordable housing, and emergency services.

Malnutrition in an Obese Nation

> Is access to food a human right? Can we morally prevent anyone in the United States from having any food because of our loyalty to capitalism?
>
> Should emergency food supplies be limited to the sporadic charity of generous people and churches?
>
> Since the vestiges of the old food stamp program come nowhere near filling the void of American food insecurity, what is the right answer for the twenty-first century?

"Bite?" It is a monosyllabic question often heard at the dinner table when my friend and I are trying to get her young grandchildren to be more interested in the food on their plates than in the toys waiting for them nearby. Their round cheeks and healthy thick bodies betray the luxury of their indifference towards their dinner. In their world, there is always more than enough, and even if they ignore dinner now, they are confident that something will be available later.

That same word, "Bite?," I've discovered, can make the world stand still when it comes from the mouth of a tiny undersized child. Most communities have a pantry program to distribute groceries to families who are facing an emergency. The reasons for the emergency in our currently blighted economy are not hard to imagine, nor should it come as a surprise that the number of families showing up at these pantry programs in severe need is steadily rising.

The poor frequently do not appear to be starving. In fact, poverty often causes both depression and bad eating habits that lead to obesity. But, in the midst of a real crisis, some people are not just eating the wrong foods, they are not eating. And so, when a very young boy looked at the bags of groceries I was carrying out to the car of a single mom making her first visit to our pantry, pointed and said "Bite?" with an intonation of hope . . . well, folks, that was just more than I could take.

In our small city we usually serve between fifty and a hundred families every day. Sometimes we have so many that I have to dip into limited church funds and go to a grocery store to buy another truckload of supplies. We try to be upbeat and encouraging to the people who are in need. There are lots of smiles and "have a nice day" and "God bless you" exchanges. We don't have time to sit and talk much during a very busy day of moving cases of canned goods and bags of frozen chicken, but as I have tried to stay in bed on a sleepless night after a day at the pantry, it is not the sore muscles from the manual labor that keeps me awake; it is the echo of a little boy asking for a bite of food.

It is said that, "Christianity gave birth to capitalism and prosperity and was, in turn, devoured by her offspring." The presence of hunger in the richest nation in the world is a moral black eye, because hunger can only exist if we choose to allow it to exist.

Capitalism, while it has been effective at creating great wealth, also has its casualties. It can kill us morally if we allow ourselves to become indifferent towards the plight of those who fall through the cracks. Giving to your local pantry program is a way to directly put food on the table where hungry children live. Still, charity cannot be the whole answer to the problem of poverty related hunger in a wealthy nation. Somehow the whole economic system must be transformed.

Minimum Wage Vs Living Wage

What does it mean for a wealthy nation to have a minimum wage
that is significantly less than what it actually takes to live?

Seattle raised its minimum wage to $15 per hour and in one year reduced its unemployment by 25 percent. Why wouldn't more municipal governments follow suit?

The prediction that raises in the minimum wage will result in job losses has been universally shown to be false, so why do so many still offer that objection?

In George Orwell's classic novel about political doublespeak, *1984*, protagonist, Winston Smith wonders if the public is told often enough that 2+2=5 would it start to believe it? If the majority of the population believes it is true, does it become true? A century before Orwell, the Russian novelist, Ivan Turgenev, similarly said about religion's denial of reality that, "Every prayer reduces itself to this: Great God, grant that two plus two not equal four."

There is no way to declare absolute truth, even in most of the sciences, and especially not in economics. The math part of economic theory would seem to be the one place where logic can be absolute, but in a culture accustomed to having the world interpreted to it through political spin, even math is subject to fanciful manipulation.

I had some courses in economics when I was in college, but my real education came in the jungles of Nicaragua as I watched the efforts of a non-governmental organization making micro-business loans, trying to create an economy where one had not previously existed. To solve poverty, people have to be able to buy and sell, which means that they must also produce and consume, because hoarding kills an economy and creates poverty.

One of the current hot topics of politics is the issue of raising the minimum wage. Any proposed change in the economy will have winners and losers. The people at the top of the economy, the current winners, never want to see a change in the rules. The increasingly impoverished middle class, currently the majority, naturally wants to see changes that would increase buying and selling, producing and consuming, unless it can be convinced, by either religion or political spin, that it should vote against its own interests in support of the status quo.

The economy is not stimulated when we take from the poor what little they have and give it to the hoarders. Yet our economic policy of cutting estate taxes, cutting capital gains taxes, and creating tax loopholes for off-shore investments is, in fact, taking from the poor to give to the rich. We have been told that these hoarders are job creators but, to believe that, we would have to also believe that two and two is something other than four.

We did not create a better economy in rural villages in Nicaragua by giving more money to the coffee plantation owners who have become wealthy on the virtual slave labor of the poor. We did it by giving small business loans to the poor and teaching them how to manufacture and market to their neighbors.

You cannot raise everyone to CEO level salaries and expect that to work, just as you cannot realistically defend the existence of a minimum wage that is below a reasonable living wage and act like you are protecting the jobs of the poor, unless, of course, you are willing to believe that two plus two, plus some hocus-pocus, and wishing will turn into a strong economy. There should be no working poor in twenty-first century America. Anyone who defends a minimum wage that is below a living wage is lacking in compassion or patriotism or—maybe just doesn't understand math.

Money Does Not Exist

> In Gene Roddenberry's conception of the Federation in Star Trek, there is no currency. Can you imagine a future in which everyone is given adequate housing, healthcare, food, clothing, and transportation without wages or any exchange of money?

> Comedian Bill Maher pointed out that you cannot oppose both an increased minimum wage and government handouts to the poor. If we will not pay people a living wage, the government must provide welfare programs. Why not simply force profitable companies to pay their own employees a living wage?

> Why do we keep fighting the minimum wage issue so often? Why not peg it to the cost of living and automatically adjust it every year so that it never gets so out of proportion to real buying power?

Money does not exist. Money is a concept. The philosopher Alan Watts used the analogy of a carpenter who came to work one day and was told that they could not finish building the house he was working on because they had run out of inches. Actual wealth resides in resources such as land, rare metals, energy sources, food, water, building materials, and vehicles.

Money is just a concept we have invented to help us to distribute real wealth. Currency only works if we agree on the system and play by the economic rules that create it.

Real wealth is created when we build something, grow something, mine something, or assemble something. Unfortunately, our economic system allows for a great deal of real wealth to be transferred into the hands of people who do not create wealth; they simply own assets or control them through financial instruments and institutions. When we have idle workers who are not building, growing, and making things, our total real wealth is going down. The best of economic systems keep people working in the creation of real wealth.

Dorothy Day, the founder of the Catholic Worker movement, preached that we need a revolution in how we think about the distribution of wealth. She said, "Our problems stem from our acceptance of this filthy, rotten system."[2]

When economic commentators insist that we cannot pay those who build, grow, or manufacture our nation's real wealth a living wage because it would "hurt the economy," then you should immediately realize that you are reading an irrational defense of a filthy, rotten economic system that discourages the creation of real wealth in favor of simply transferring existing wealth into the hands of fewer and fewer people.

Those who resist raises to the minimum wage or who insist upon legislation that undermines the unions that protect worker's jobs, wages, and benefits often cite studies that conclude that it is the greed of teachers, fire fighters, labor union members, and selfish young people who want to go to college that is threatening our economic future. They use these studies, as Paul Krugman says, "the way a drunk uses a lamppost – for support, not for illumination."[3]

The stock market continues to climb to new heights, making the rich ever richer, while real wealth remains stagnant or, in fact, is declining, eroding the middle class and undermining the economic future of our nation. We have been sold a malignant myth that wealthy people are job creators. Demand in the marketplace is what creates jobs, and demand comes as more people are able to buy things.

Still, the far right cries out against labor unions and a president that they insist upon labeling "socialist," while our nation's existing wealth

2. Day, Wikiquote
3. Krugman, "Fiscal Fever Breaks."

continues to be handed over to the super rich, and the middle class disappears before our eyes. What system works to create wealth and bolster the middle class? Economist Robert Reich has a very plausible answer: the system employed in the United States of America between 1947 and 1977, when we built America's middle class and created the standard of living that was the envy of the world.[4] That system had much more successful collection of corporate taxes and a graduated tax code that forced the wealthy to pay a larger percentage on their income than their less wealthy employees. Or, to say it in another way, the opposite of what we are doing now.

Anyone who says our future must include a continuing transfer of wealth to the super rich while impoverishing the creators of wealth is not deserving of serious consideration.

Burning Down Our House While We Are Still in It

How many pairs of shoes did you own thirty years ago? How many pairs of shoes do you own now? Did you feel deprived when you only owned four or five pairs of shoes? Can you imagine returning to that number of shoes in your current lifestyle?

Older homes have smaller closets than newer homes. How did families manage with only four or five changes of clothes?

If a product produced in China costs a fourth of what the same product costs produced locally, even after having been transported half way around the globe, what must the income of the people who produced those goods be?

To survive in extreme cold, people might be driven to break up and burn their furniture to stay warm. They may even be reduced to pulling the wood from the walls of their cabin to keep a fire going, but if the cold weather persists, this technique will end up leaving the person both homeless and freezing. When it comes to economics, we want to avoid having to burn our own house down to stay alive.

The demise of locally-owned retail stores in favor of discount chains puts us daily in the position of shopping for necessities at the lowest price possible while draining our economy of the capital with which to buy those necessities next week. Like a lot of progressives, I have avoided doing

4. Reich, "Why Inequality is the Real Cause of Our Ongoing Terrible Economy."

business with Wal-Mart as often as possible, but I have come to accept that Wal-Mart is so deeply rooted in the world economy that it no longer makes sense to try to stop its spread.

As a person who is concerned about the economy on behalf of the poor, my energy has shifted from trying to starve Wal-Mart out of existence to wanting to change Wal-Mart's employment practices. If I could persuade our neighbors in Bentonville to seriously look at the employment practices of one of its last surviving competitors, Costco, then I believe that there are some changes that Wal-Mart could make that would not only benefit its millions of employees and thousands of cities and towns where it does business, these changes also benefit Wal-Mart's bottom line. Wal-Mart has been so obsessed with keeping prices low that it pays the lowest possible salaries, and that inevitably means that it is impoverishing its customer base and burning down the economy where it hopes to make a profit.

Harvard Business Review took a wide-angle look at the competitors in 2006 noting that, at that time, Costco's average worker salary was $17 per hour and Wal-Mart's was about $10. Costco also provided their employees more benefits in healthcare and retirement. The higher salary at Costco resulted in higher worker retention and productivity resulting in employee costs that were actually lower than Wal-Mart's. This allows Costco to offer virtually the same price on goods as Wal-Mart while also making a higher profit.[5]

Of course, we might always prefer to buy locally grown and produced foods, but these choices are often limited to those who can afford to pay the inevitable premium price we encounter in locally owned stores and farmers' markets. Still, it has always been a cherished value among people of conscience to try to live more simply and to be consumers who employ not only economic savvy but who also buy with both awareness and conscience.

America's Northern Test Kitchen

> Americans spend about $10,000 per student in public education. Since not sending your child to public school saves the education system that amount of money, should parents be allowed to have the same amount of money contributed on their child's behalf to a private school?

5. Cascio, "The High Cost of Low Wages."

The state is obliged to provide a free public education to children within their school districts, but to what extent does the state have the right to impose a secular curriculum on these schools?

The general public has an interest in making certain that the next generation is well-educated, but in a public vs private contest where the public interest conflicts with parents' desire to give their children a specific religious education, how do we choose a winner?

The sheer enormity and diversity of the American population contributes to what is making our nation both a superpower and supremely inefficient. Managing unemployment, healthcare delivery, and education wouldn't be difficult if only we were a nation of three hundred thousand rather than a population of three hundred million. And so we look to smaller nations as being a sort of laboratory experiment for what works and what doesn't work as we drag our collective knuckles into the twenty-first century.

In spite of misleading anecdotal stories, our neighbors to the north have managed to create a national healthcare service that manages costs much better than we do and covers everyone rather than just the majority, as ours does. I realize that there are Americans who prefer to have better care than what they might have in a national healthcare system, even if that means millions must go without adequate healthcare, but I refuse to accept that such moral midgets should get to have their way in a matter where so very much is at stake. The "I got mine" argument is so bereft of nobility as to be undeserving of consideration.

But while Canadians have national healthcare, they have gone in the other direction in education. Private schools in Canada receive public funds in a voucher system much the way that many conservatives have suggested for our schools. As we have lately been treated to how disastrous it is to have a church in charge of healthcare policy via the Catholic Church's objections to allowing women the same healthcare coverage they are afforded in secular settings, Canada is now discovering what a negative influence religion can have on education.

The liberal Ontario government has recently passed an anti-bullying measure similar to what is being enacted in school systems throughout the western world. And, of course, it includes protections of gay students from bullying.[6] After all, who would be in favor of bullying a student for being

6. Mallick, "Ontario's new anti-bullying 'gay-straight' law was born of heroism."

gay? (Please note the tongue-in-cheek reference to Mitt Romney). What Toronto residents were surprised to learn is that none other than their own Catholic Archbishop, Cardinal Thomas Collins, vociferously objects to the protection of gay students from bullying in Catholic schools.[7] The blatant hypocrisy of the Archbishop has created a public outcry to remove public funds from private schools).

Americans would do well to look to our neighbors to the north to learn some important lessons: Using vouchers to transfer funds from public schools to private religious schools is bad for public schools, bad for students subjected to prejudiced religious education, and bad for minorities. Therefore, I submit, we shouldn't do it.

If we are paying attention to the facts rather than the partisan rhetoric, we can also learn from our own mistake of leaving the management of healthcare in the hands of employers. This is especially so when the employer is a religious institution rife with restrictive views on the rights of a minority (in this case, women of childbearing age). Some things are just better done collectively than privately.

The Imperfect Science of Economics

What do you think it would take to spark an economic revolution in America, transferring a more significant amount of the income produced in our country into the hands of the middle and lower economic classes?

Since trickle-down economics has clearly not worked over the past thirty years in our country, what kind of political will is necessary to rebalance the tax burden?

Taxes are, by definition, a redistribution of wealth. Can we devise a tax code that does not punish the poor for being poor and that does not allow wealth to be hoarded in a way that impoverishes most people?

Warren Buffett created a stir in the billionaires' club when he told a New York Times reporter that America is in the midst of class warfare, and that the rich are winning. Buffett made this comment as deregulation in the banking industry, tax cuts for the rich, and runaway spending on Middle

7. Southey, "Archbishop Chooses the Wrong Cause to Play the Martyr."

Eastern wars were setting the world up for a global recession. The predictable economic collapse which was made inevitable by tax cuts, wars, and deregulation was deepened by political leaders who insisted that the way out of this disaster was—and please try to resist sticking a sharp stick in your eye when you read this—by more tax cuts for the wealthy, further deregulation, and doubling down on our war in Afghanistan. Yeah, I know.

The reporter who made a prank phone call to the Wisconsin governor, Scott Walker, pretending to be one of his super wealthy donors made it obvious that the battle between Walker and the people who make his state work is not about balancing the state budget, but about breaking the labor unions that protect the lower middle class from becoming peasants. The transcript of that prank phone call is a sobering reminder of how unapologetically the rich and powerful plan to gut the standard of living of the state's workers while shamefully planning unethical junkets for themselves.

Watching the social upheaval in Tunisia, Egypt, Bahrain, and Syria during the Arab spring, it was not difficult to see the demonstrations in Wisconsin just as Republican Senator Paul Ryan described them: "It's like Cairo has moved to Madison," drawing a parallel between his governor and Hosni Mubarak.

However unintended, the comparison was appropriate as the poor will eventually organize to throw off their political and economic oppressors. Strangely, however, in the United States, anti-union sentiment remains strong even among those who would most likely benefit from collective bargaining, proving conclusively that you can sell snowballs to Eskimos if you insist that not buying the snowballs makes one an unpatriotic, socialist atheist.

Congressional Budget Office figures demonstrate that over the past thirty years, the share of the wealth produced in America paid to the middle and lower class has gone down between ten to thirty percent (with an even steeper decline for the bottom rungs of our economic ladder) while the share of wealth going to the top twenty percent has risen by nearly thirty percent, and for the top one percent of Americans it has risen by nearly 130 percent. So the numbers are in: the poor are becoming poorer and the rich are rocketing up the money scale. Should we break the unions and take away worker health benefits, pensions, and job security so that we can escalate our race toward becoming just like Egypt and Syria?

The very wealthy will always exploit the talent and labor of the middle class, but if we allow them to win the class war outright, the parasites will kill the host, and then even the parasites die. There is no American democracy without a strong middle class.

The Payday Loan Nightmare

> Congress passed a law preventing payday loan companies from giving high-interest loans to active duty servicemen. If it is obvious that these predatory loans are bad for soldiers, why isn't it obvious that they are bad for everyone?

> The wealthy can usually get a two or three percent interest loan to buy a luxury car while the poor often have to pay in excess of 450 percent on a loan for emergency medical care. Shouldn't there be a more reasonable credit source for those in dire circumstances?

> Usury laws protect the public from outrageous interest rates but in many states, these laws do not apply to loans for $500 or less. While a small, short-term loan is obviously going to come at a higher interest rate, is there any justification for that rate ever exceeding 50 percent?

Our liberties are often restricted to protect social or individual wellbeing. For example, the United States has very liberal gun laws, allowing private citizens to own many more kinds of weapons than are legal in most countries but even here we don't allow a private citizen to collect mortar rounds or hand grenades. I have no doubt that a lot of people would buy them if they were available and that it would be a profitable business if you could set up a Grenades-R-Us shop, but it wouldn't be prudent. Not every decision should be based on profitability.

During Prohibition the sale of alcohol for anything other than religious services was illegal, which certainly increased attendance at synagogues and churches, but, eventually, we changed our minds about the wisdom of such laws. You used to be able to buy opium at your local drug store but for the good of both individuals and society as a whole, but we no longer allow the legal sale of narcotics. So the pendulum swings.

Libertarians question the necessity of criminalizing such things as prostitution and marijuana, but to date, the general consensus in most states is that for both individual and public welfare, we don't want to license, regulate, and tax brothels and cannabis dealers. Similarly, many states have passed legislation outlawing the existence of payday loan businesses that charge exploitative interest rates ranging from triple digit percentages all the way up to nearly 2000 percent.

No state takes as much reprehensible advantage of the desperate poor (fueling drug, alcohol, and gambling addictions) with easy-to-get but hard-to-pay-back loans as the state of Missouri. Our inability to curb this morally embarrassing industry is the direct result of campaign donations made to state legislators and municipal governments who are unwilling to cross the influential families who own these very profitable businesses.

I have noticed that during my twenty-year long public campaign against this industry, that everyone who has written into the paper to contradict my essays has been from out of state. No local owners or investors ever stands up to defend these predatory lenders because they don't want to have to go back and sit in their church pew or non-profit board seat with everyone knowing how disgustingly they have obtained their wealth.

I have given up on our governor and legislature ever mustering the political courage to do what has been done in our neighboring states. Missouri continues to grind the poor to make bread for the rich without regard for individual or public welfare. Perhaps it is time for federal legislation to do for states what some states are not willing to do for themselves.

5

Environment and Agriculture

*No excuses about being "bad for business" or "hurting jobs"
can justify making the planet uninhabitable!*

What Would Jesus Drive?

> For those of us who live in parts of the country where there are
> few or no mass transit options, how can you get to work, school,
> the grocery store, and the doctor's office with the least amount of
> damage to the environment?
>
> Everyone who lives above the tropics has to sometimes face cold
> weather driving, but how many weeks of the year do you actually
> need to drive an "all-wheel drive" vehicle the size of a small living
> room to get to work?
>
> If everyone else would do the same, would you be willing to drive
> a very small car most of the time?

"Cars are like golf clubs; you need one of every kind," a good friend told me.
On most days I travel alone and will not need to carry more than what I can
put in a small backpack. However, there are days when I have between one
and several passengers. Once a week, I need to drive a truck to take food
and supplies to feed my homeless friends. Sometimes I have to haul cases of
coats and shoes to be used either in our community or in rural Nicaragua.

My friend lives in a country home where he keeps bicycles, motorcycles, a two-seat sports car, a pickup truck and a full-sized auto. Most of us

have to choose between one or two of those vehicle options. Consequently, because we need the hauling capacity of a truck one or two days a week, many of us end up driving an SUV even when a very small car would suffice. As Robert Kennedy, Jr. has observed, "We end up taking a 500 pound power plant with us every time we go to the store to pick up five pounds of groceries."

I have tried every option from electric cars, motorcycles, and bicycles to SUVs, station wagons, and a pickup truck. I still have not found the right option to meet my needs while leaving my conscience unmolested. There is a greeting among motorcycle riders that involves pointing at the ground when you see another cyclist. I asked my cycling friends what the meaning of this gesture is, and no one has yet given me a satisfactory answer. And so I have assigned this gesture the meaning that pleases me. I see it as being reflective of the "earth witness" posture of the Buddha, in which he is sitting in the lotus position with one hand in his lap and the other extending one finger to touch the earth. This image is intended to call upon nature to bear testimony to the truth of Buddhist enlightenment.

On days when I can leave my gas-guzzling vehicles behind and ride my bike or a motorcycle, I feel a certain spiritual connection to nature, and I can point caringly at the earth, with a sincere desire to pollute less, burn up less fossil fuel, and leave a smaller carbon footprint on my way to work. If cities would provide safer bike routes for willing bike commuters, then more of us could eschew fossil fuels as often as possible.

Our irresponsible "drill, baby, drill" mentality is poisoning our only planet. Hydrogen fuel cells hold some promise and improvements in battery technology and increasing use of solar panels and wind-generated electricity will make electric cars and bikes more viable. But until alternative energy sources are common, we must all strive to reconnect with the earth and preserve as much of its resources as possible. That will mean carefully considering what kind of vehicles we purchase and use most often. Thoughtful people must be willing to suffer a certain amount of discomfort and inconvenience for the good of our "Mother."

Thinking about Eating

> Just ten companies control a huge percentage of the food supply
> you find at your local grocery store. Shouldn't our food chain be
> more diverse?[1]

> Big food corporations have a history of working to prevent ac-
> curate labeling of genetically modified foods and even some food
> additives. If we are going to have food labels at all, shouldn't they
> all be accurate?[2]

> While nutritionists advise us all to eat more fresh vegetables and
> fruits and to cut back on meat, dairy, and grains the federal gov-
> ernment is still subsidizing beef, dairy, wheat, corn, soy, rice, and
> peanuts. The wheels of government turn slowly, but don't we need
> to make it more financially possible for the poor to eat a more
> healthy diet?[3]

Many of us who grew up in farming areas have long abandoned our agricultural roots, swapping tomatoes and beans for petunias and iris beds.
For reasons of health, economics, and the environment, maybe it would
be a good thing for us to try to rekindle our connection with the earth, the
source of everything we eat.

Garrison Keillor has written about that time in late summer when the
residents of the fictional community of Lake Wobegon have to start locking
their car and kitchen doors to keep neighbors from dropping off unsolicited grocery bags of green peppers, squash, and cucumbers that grow in
abundance that time of the year. Sure, anyone can grow zucchini, but it
doesn't actually translate into real food . . . you can batter and fry it so that
it tastes like a damp hushpuppy, or you can grate it up and bake it in bread,
but if you add the same amount of grass clippings and a half a cup of water
to the recipe, it would turn out about the same.

But no one ever turns away a gift of dinner table staples such as potatoes, corn, green beans, peas, lettuce, or melons. Now, when many poverty-
related organizations are reporting that donations are down and demand
for food assistance is up, I believe that we should all try to make a new effort

1. Bradford, "These 10 Companies Control Enormous Number of Consumer
Brands."

2. Maheshwari and Sanders, "Big Food Is Quietly Spending Millions To Prevent
GMO Labeling In The U.S."

3. Mercola, "The 9 Foods the U.S. Government is Paying You to Eat."

toward growing edible crops, not just for ourselves, but to donate to home-less shelters and food programs. Fresh, locally-grown produce will always be welcomed at these agencies that help to stave off hunger among the poor while improving the nutritional habits of children.

Re-learning the skills necessary to produce edible agricultural prod-ucts is good for our own health, as we can add more fresh fruits and veg-etables to our family's diet and avoid the chemical additives that are almost always a part of produce sold in stores.

Growing more food locally is also good for the environment in that locally produced agricultural products do not come with the huge carbon footprint associated with transporting food from hundreds of miles away. Also, the more farm labor that can be done with hand tools reduces the amount of petroleum used in major farming operations. Sadly, even the small tillers used in domestic gardens are often the most fuel-inefficient and carbon waste-producing motors in use today, as are most of our lawn mowers.

Backyard gardening is good for our health, our environment, and for the agencies that depend upon donations of food. Take a moment to look at the seeds offered at local greenhouses and picture yourself in overalls, pitchfork in hand, and working for the good of America.

Short Term Thinking in the Energy Industry

Some industries see their demise coming in inevitable ways. The automobile killed the covered wagon industry and computers eliminated the need for slide-rules but others put themselves out of business by failing to change with market needs. The coal and oil industry has grown huge on decades of obscene profits but their product is killing their customers. Will energy companies successfully transition to investing heavily in alternative energy or will they have to be forced to stop poisoning our only planet?

The transition to solar and wind energy will require substantial investment in infrastructure. Should we wait for private industry to make that investment or should states and/or the federal gov-ernment take the lead?

If the federal government subsidized the manufacture of solar panels and wind turbines in areas where coal jobs were ending, would you support a government initiative to make such a seamless transition from fossil fuels to renewables?

Imagine a lifeboat quickly sinking in rough seas with ten passengers trying to make it safely to shore. Six people are rowing the boat through the swells, two are bailing out the ever-rising water from the boat, and the other two are busy drilling holes in the bottom of the boat.

What should be done to get the boat and its passengers to safety? Should the six who are rowing work harder? Should the two who are bailing work faster? Sadly, as this question has been posed to the United States Congress our legislators have done everything but ask the two who are drilling holes in the hull to stop. Perhaps this is because big oil and big coal companies think they own the boat. What they never seem to understand is that the short-term profits that kill off the planet means that the very corporations that are sinking our lifeboat will inevitably drown.

Each successive summer seems to be the hottest on record. As the seas heat up, hurricanes become more frequent and more deadly, and freshwater lakes are disappearing while other parts of the world are being flooded.

Africa's Lake Chad, which covered nearly 10,000 square miles a few years ago and provided water and a livelihood to millions of people in four nations is now down to only 500 square miles and may be entirely gone in another year or two. The same may now be happening to the lakes that provide water to Atlanta. This is lethal and there is no time to waste in reversing the trend. Our dependence upon carbon-based fuels (gasoline and electricity generated by burning coal) is sinking our only boat.

Many Republicans still deny that human activity is negatively affecting the earth's temperature. Though Democrats pay lip service to the issues of global climate change, they have accomplished little more than their climate-denying rivals.

Conservation and symbolic efforts at alternative energy will not prevent the irretrievable sinking of the environment. No excuses about being "bad for business" or "hurting jobs" can justify making the planet uninhabitable!

Should We Fear Frankenfoods?

Lobbyists for the American dairy industry prevailed upon Congress to allow them not to mention the fact that they put artificial

sweeteners in milk. If food products are required to list ingredients on the label, shouldn't they be required to list all added
ingredients?

Identifying foods with genetically modified ingredients is common in most countries, but often made illegal in the United States.
Do you feel you have a right to know?

Should our federal food subsidies be shifted away from foods that
aren't as good for us (i.e., corn, wheat, rice, soy, and potatoes) and
toward more fruits and green vegetables?

Through social connections, I have spent a good deal of time in the university labs and around the scientists who work on agricultural research.
If you can modify a potato vine to not be susceptible to certain viruses, or
alter wheat so that it has a shorter and stronger stalk that will not be easily
blown down in the wind, or make corn that needs less water, or soy beans
that yield more at harvest time, then the world's food supply is increased
and farmers can make more profits.

For the most part, these agricultural scientists have been a blessing to
our world, which now feeds an unimaginably large population, but there
is a down side. Human life is now nearly entirely dependent upon nutrition from five primary crops: corn, wheat, rice, soy, and potatoes. What if
our tinkering with the genetic makeup of these crops should result in one
or two of them becoming lost in the sort of global blight that killed the
American Chestnut tree? Just take either rice or wheat out of the equation,
and the world would face a threat of mass starvation.

On a few occasions, sitting around a backyard picnic table with a
group of agricultural scientists, I brought up the word "nutrition." I was
surprised at how angry very smart people can become at the mention of
something as crucial to food as its nutritional value. There are instances of
genetically modified foods having an apparent increase in nutritional value
but more appear to have much less, and some have virtually none.[4]

GMOs (genetically modified organisms) can be toxic, and can cause
food allergies. There has been relatively little testing done on humans, and
yet these products are reaching our store shelves. In the United States,
foods containing GMO ingredients are not labeled as they are in Europe
and even in China.

4. Brown, "GMO Myths and Truths."

In our country, where democracy is demonstrably for sale, giant food corporations have so much influence on our government that we continue to subsidize the foods that make us fat and diabetic and give us heart disease, but we do not subsidize production of the foods that would make us healthier. We have given research grants to create these "frankenfoods" and then protected manufacturers from legal liability for the problems they create.

The reason people all over America are participating in March Against Monsanto events is because this single corporate entity is directly responsible for many of the most outrageous abuses in removing government oversight from the production of food. Despite a great deal of public protest, President Obama appointed a Monsanto vice president to be the chief advisor to our Food and Drug Administration, a move that left me in shock. No one in his or her right mind would have appointed a fox to guard this crucial henhouse unless forced to do so. Apparently, Monsanto is more powerful than the government of the United States, and that should not be something we silently accept.

Victory Gardens in the Twenty-First Century

Do you grow edible produce in your own yard? Do you know how?

If your garden produced much more than your family could use, do you know how to get the extra food to a poverty-related program?

If your church were willing to plant a garden to produce food for the poor, would you volunteer to work in the garden?

The sweet taste of concord grapes instantly transports me back to my favorite uncle's garden, where helping him to pick his precious grapes was a childhood delight. But you won't find these gems in a chain grocery store. You will find them at open-air farmers' markets and specialty shops dealing in locally grown produce. Talking with the growers as you stroll through the open-air market you can taste a variety of sweet corn that is delicious to eat raw—just pull off the shucks and discover what raccoons have known for centuries—this stuff doesn't need to be boiled, buttered or salted!

Shopping at our local farmers' markets is good for the environment, good for local farmers, good for consumers' health and, well, it tastes good! It takes more time because there is no purposeful organization as to how products are displayed and there is not a singular checkout stand. You have to go through several individual transactions before heading home. But bigger than the time issue is that this wonderful, healthy, tasty, and environmentally friendly food is a lot more expensive than what you can buy elsewhere, making it more a luxury purchase for the middle and upper class than a practical choice for the poor.

We are now, for the first time in history, facing an epidemic of obesity among the poor, along with its companions: diabetes and heart disease. This is so because the cheapest foods available to the disadvantaged are often the absolute worst of processed, high calorie, sugar, fat, and salt-riddled packaged foods. As I walked through the aisles at our Council of Churches food pantry, helping an economically destitute family select three days' worth of emergency groceries, I was pleased that fresh produce, milk, and eggs were on the list, but a lot of the packaged foods were not what I would personally eat or serve to my family.

For the past few years at my church, we kept a garden plot on our property to grow fresh produce that we either give to poverty food programs or we prepare ourselves to serve to the unsheltered homeless. There are several national programs encouraging people to grow fresh produce in their own yards to share with the poor, but these efforts seem to be merely symbolic in terms of how much food is being produced.

So, I have some modest proposals:

1. Support your local growers by shopping at your farmers' markets.

2. Local growers should support our local poverty programs by donating excess produce.

3. If you possibly can, plant fruit and nut trees on your property. Plant a garden. Eat healthy food from your own garden and donate as much as you can.

4. I encourage churches to actively participate in this effort: Grow food on your church property as an example to your members and consider offering classes in canning and drying foods to share throughout the year.

6

Healthcare

If America is the patient, I'm going to say that the patient has a serious heart problem, or maybe an entirely missing heart.

Henhouse Security in the Hands of the Foxes

Is access to healthcare a human right, or is it a commodity that you have a right to only if you can afford to pay for it?

In most professional fields, there are extensive conversations about "best practices." What are the best practices of nations that are successful in healthcare delivery and cost management?

The very wealthy will always have access to the best healthcare in the world. But given that society has a vested economic and moral interest in the health and productivity of the entire population, should there be a basic healthcare program that includes everyone?

In the midst of the healthcare debate around the Affordable Care Act, I attended a meeting in one of the most unlikely places for me to show up—the local Chamber of Commerce. They were true to their reputation for upholding a right wing, pro-business perspective when they invited a member of Congress, the CEOs of two local hospitals, and an insurance executive to lead the discussion.

All of the speakers acknowledged the necessity of covering the uninsured and lowering costs, but none were willing to recommend any radical change. It was like listening to a panel of foxes bemoaning how many chickens were missing from the hen house, while firmly asserting that nothing must be substantively changed in hen house security.

We have some hard facts to face. Political campaigns are partially, and sometimes primarily, financed by insurance and pharmaceutical company donations. Not-for-profit hospitals own for-profit insurance companies that are bottom-line and market-share driven. Asking owners and managers of insurance companies and politicians who take money from the insurance industry to tell us how to fix healthcare is not a reasonable way to manage the huge crisis of healthcare costs and access to care. These are the people who will only get to keep robbing the hen house if the system remains broken.

The hospital administrators also decried long waits in emergency rooms and the problems of the uninsured, but were more interested in congratulating themselves on the medical miracles performed in their operating rooms every day than in suggesting how the system can be changed to expand coverage and lower costs.

The speakers frequently referred to the 83 percent of Americans who have healthcare coverage, as if to say that since only one in five Americans isn't covered, then the problem is not really all that bad. As stunningly heartless as that attitude is, it also fails to take into consideration the very basic fact that many of those who are insured have had to accept higher deductibles in order to keep their insurance premium low enough to still be able to buy groceries. Once you have a deductible of $5000, as I did before Obamacare, are you really insured? What we really have is catastrophic insurance, but unless you have a heart attack or a serious car accident, any visit to the doctor comes straight out of a wallet already emptied by paying hundreds of dollars each month for insurance that is useless unless you are near death.

My doctor has been telling me for the past few years that guys my age should have a colonoscopy, which would cost me about $3000. Should I spend that amount of money on a test to see if I have cancer or should I go ahead and send my daughter back to college this fall? That's what it is like for many of us to be "insured!"

Nearly one-fifth of our nation's economy is consumed by healthcare, and those costs continued rising rapidly until the introduction of the Affordable Care Act. There is no permanent solution to this crisis as long as insurance companies survive the reform. The Obama plan isn't perfect, but what we were offered by our local congress member and friends was just another rearrangement of the deck chairs on the Titanic.

Seeing Both Sides of the Abortion Debate

> To reduce the number of abortions in America is it better to make abortions more difficult to obtain or make birth control easier to obtain?

> Does society have a responsibility to protect children from the violence of poverty?

> Do people have a right to expect public assistance for the expenses related to raising children?

One of the beautiful things about high school and college debate is that it teaches students to think logically about both sides of a complicated issue. Every team has to prepare both pro and con arguments with equal zeal, because the team does not know until the day of the debate which position they will have to defend. Controversial issues are controversial because there are entirely logical and sound reasons to take either side on the matter.

I wish that everyone involved in the abortion debate could have the experience of being forced to enthusiastically argue both sides of the issue. For my entire adult life, we've been hurling the same bits of "evidence" at one another, yet it hardly seems that anyone on either side is ever listening. I appreciate the religious defense of the sanctity of life, and I see the hypocrisy of placing a high moral value on the life of the unborn while doing so little to show similar concern for the millions of children who have been born who are inadequately housed, fed, educated, or medically cared for.

I can see how that those who believe that not-yet-born have the same human rights as those of us who have been born view our country's abortion laws as a virtual condoning of a daily holocaust. And yet, when abortion was illegal in the United States, it created a two-tiered system of justice in which those who could afford the gas or a plane ticket to another country could easily obtain an abortion, while the poor were forced to either live out the moral convictions of those who were in power or take unspeakable risks in illegal abortion methods.

Most people are not actually opposed to abortion in all cases. Most people are opposed to other people getting abortions, but almost everyone believes that he or she is personally capable of making appropriate moral decisions about when abortion should be an option for a member of her or his own family.

Politicians who reject political pressure to try to take control of the bedroom and the wombs of voters may not win many Tea Party votes, but I believe that whether or not voters are willing to admit it publicly, pro-choice politicians come much closer to the heart of the way most of us really feel.

Very few people are "pro-abortion." Most of us believe that abortions should be safe, legal, and rare. There are circumstances in which the most moral choice in a morally convoluted situation is to terminate a pregnancy, and I believe that in almost every case, the decision should be made by the woman, and not by the vote or the religious convictions of her neighbors.

Whether you are entirely pro-choice or entirely anti-abortion, there is a clear common ground where both can meet, and that is trying to make abortion a less attractive option. Abortions become less frequent when young mothers have the economic resources to raise a family. Political decisions that make child rearing for the poor more difficult, such as cutting food stamp programs, failing to subsidized child care, choosing not to expand Medicaid, and not providing after school programs, have a direct connection to the number of pregnancies terminated in America.

The Inevitability of a National Healthcare System

National healthcare programs are the norm in most industrialized nations. If the same is an inevitable reality in the United States, has the Affordable Care Act delayed the inevitable or has it been a necessary first step in that direction?

Would you favor a stepped-in expansion of Medicare, lowering the age of eligibility a few years at a time until it is comprehensive?

Would you prefer an expansion of Medicaid that only offered healthcare to the poor but left those who can buy private health insurance free to either acquire insurance or take the risk of going without coverage?

"My dad is a doctor but not the kind that can help anybody." My daughter's explanation of my academic title to her preschool playmate stung a little but I knew what she meant. Some of her friends had parents who were the kind of doctors who gave sick people medicine and somehow they were real doctors and I was just a talking doctor.

But after twenty-five years of carrying the title while not being able to write a prescription, I now feel compelled to enter the arena of medicine and issue a doctor's diagnosis. If America is the patient, I'm going to say that the patient has a serious heart problem, or maybe an entirely missing heart. Listening for the sound of a pulse, I have heard people gloating about the failed launch of the website for Obamacare. I have heard ridiculous and dishonest allegations of socialism, communism and the frightening specter of death panels and the rationing of healthcare.

What I don't hear are two parties debating how best to deliver healthcare in the most effective and economically efficient manner possible to the people who need it. The primary issue that isn't being mentioned is that, according to research published in the New England Journal of Medicine, an estimated 45,000 Americans die every year as a direct result of not having adequate health insurance.[1]

That's more than die from automobile accidents, or gunshot wounds, terrorism, or wars. That is 45,000 entirely preventable deaths if we would only find the heart to do what almost every other industrialized nation in the world has already done. While political rhetoric still insists that we have the best healthcare in the world, the fact is that we only have the best if what you mean by best is "the most expensive." We are near the bottom of the list in infant mortality among industrialized nations.[2]

We spend more on healthcare than any other nation in the world and yet we are ranked thirty-eighth in overall healthcare, far below the nations that have national healthcare programs.[3]

You don't like Obamacare? Well, let me go on the record as one bleeding-heart liberal who agrees with you. Obamacare is a halfway measure cooked up in a conservative Republican think tank, the Heritage Foundation. It is a means of forcing[4] more people to turn over their resources to insurance companies that, like me, don't actually diagnosis illnesses, perform surgeries, prescribe medications, or even empty bedpans, but that, unlike me, take billions of dollars out of healthcare to pay enormous salaries to their executives and dividends to their stockholders.

1. Tailor and Stillman, "Dead Man Walking."
2. Wikipedia, "List of Countries by Infant Mortality Rate"
3. Wikipedia, "World Health Organization Ranking of Health Systems."
4. Taranto, "Heritage Rewrites History."

The problem with Obamacare is that it is designed to protect insurance company profits more than to do what anyone with a heart in her or his chest should want the most, give healthcare to people who need it. America will end up with a universal healthcare program. It is inevitable because anything else will bankrupt our economy. Obamacare is a step in the direction of universal healthcare . . . A poorly conceived, inefficient and embarrassing step, but a necessary one.

The only question now is just how many people are we willing to allow to die from want of appropriate medical attention before we get to where we know that we have to go?

A Fair Distribution of Healthcare

> Should Medicare, Medicaid, private insurance, and the choice to be uninsured be rolled into a single payer, national healthcare system similar to the healthcare programs in most western nations?

> Should insurance and pharmaceutical companies be able to legally make political contributions to the politicians who regulate their industries?

> Is it right for the governor of one state to choose to expand Medicaid and another sate's governor to choose not to expand Medicaid when the welfare of so many indigent citizens is at stake?

> Have you known anyone who has died because she or he was denied proper healthcare? Have you known anyone who has had to take bankruptcy or who has committed suicide because of medical bills? If you did, would it change how you feel about our national healthcare system?

Imagine, if you will, that a ship carrying one hundred passengers is shipwrecked on an isolated island. Imagine as well that on board that ship there was a doctor, an architect, a dentist, an engineer, a seamstress, some farmers, some builders, maybe a barber, some educators, an interior decorator, and a preacher.

This small community of one hundred souls must now build housing, provide food, medical care, education, water, and maybe a source of heat as well as haircuts, religious services and some esthetic arrangement of rocks and plants for themselves. In building this society would you expect that 90 percent of the food would be given to thirty people or that the doctor would treat seventy-five of the island's residents and ignore the other twenty-five?

Of course not, nor would the barber cut only fifty heads of hair. And, I suspect that the preacher would swear that he had two hundred people in Sunday services every week. The problem with our delivery of housing, food, water, medical care, and education is that it was not a system that was logically designed for efficiency and fairness in the twenty-first century, but rather it all evolved over long periods of time under circumstances that were dramatically different from our situation today.

Consider the healthcare system set up by our government in Iraq after we had bombed their hospital and clinic system out of existence. As we have attempted to give the gift of democracy to the Iraqis we have not, at the same time, given them a healthcare system that includes competing insurance companies and various levels of care for persons in different classes, nor have we left 20 percent of the Iraqi population out of the healthcare system as we have in the United States.

During World War II, when there was a wage and price freeze in the United States, employers began offering health insurance as an incentive to attract employees from a smaller workforce. This untaxed benefit then became a staple of employment in the 1950s that funded the rise of our health insurance companies and influenced the ways hospitals and doctors offered their services.

What made sense in 1945 is massively ignorant in the twenty-first century. We have the most expensive, unfair, and illogical healthcare system in the world. If we had created a national healthcare system in the 1990s when President Clinton tried to get the system reformed, we would have more competitively priced manufactured goods and there would be a logical and understandable distribution of healthcare.

President Obama attempted to get the wheels of reform rolling to help to deliver healthcare to sick people without bankrupting them. The insurance companies put more than $100 million into stopping any reform of the current system. Clearly, the insurance industry is willing to wring every dime of profit it can out of this nation, even if it has to kill us in the process.

If we think in terms of the microcosm of a hundred people living on an island, the ethical questions come into focus pretty readily. All one hundred people should receive relatively similar attention to their needs, regardless of preexisting conditions, age, skin color, or economic class. The ethics would be the same when you apply it to a nation of three hundred million people. It is admittedly more complicated to administer, but the degree of complication doesn't really change the ethical dynamics.

Suicide and Medical Bills

> Have you ever contemplated suicide due to economic circumstances beyond your control? Can you sympathize with those who have?
>
> Having a medical emergency can be like writing a blank check to a hospital that has no compunction about billing you much more than you could possibly pay. Should we protect citizens from catastrophic healthcare bills?
>
> If compassion is integral to the message of all major religions, why is it that we don't see more compassion in nations where religious practice is more common?

The mortality rate is 100 percent. Everybody dies and in most cases a preacher is involved in the final ceremony. Some funerals are harder than others. The death of an infant, or a murder resulting from domestic violence, or a teen auto accident, create such traumatic feelings of loss that the memorial service itself becomes a supercharged event out of which we pastors hope to deliver some comfort, assurance, and hope of eventual healing.

The hardest services for me are the deaths by suicide. People can feel driven to the point of taking their own lives because they have a problem that they cannot solve and with which they choose not to live—chronic depression that doesn't respond to treatment, addiction that won't let go, divorce, the specter of past abuse, rejection by loved ones because of one's sexual orientation—all can make death look like a good option. I have presided over those services to the best of my ability and have eventually been able to accept the sad but unavoidable fact of their deaths.

My most recent funeral for a suicide victim was the most difficult one of my long career. It is the first time I've had to deal in a personal way with a death from a failure of politics. Kevin was laid off from his job and, in this economy, he simply couldn't find another one. Of course, since in our country, health insurance is usually tied to work, Kevin was uninsured when the stress of unemployment caused him to have a heart attack. Medical science saved his life. Stents were put in place to open closed arteries.

He was released from the hospital, alive but unable to work at the age of forty-nine.

Not being able to work does not mean that Social Security cannot deny your application for disability. Being unemployed and disabled doesn't keep the hospital from turning your $70,000 in medical bills over to bill collectors. Yes, it was Kevin who turned a gun on himself, but social forces beyond his control caused his death.

Insurance lobbyists made sure that healthcare reform ended up not giving America the kind of universal healthcare embraced in every other industrialized nation. Kevin took his life because our Congress has failed to pass a job creation bill that would have put young, productive, talented workers back on the job. This suicide was the direct result of an insane, indefensible, and cruel healthcare delivery system that is sucking the life out of America.

The deepest cut for me is the awareness that in nations where church attendance is almost undetectable, there is yet a level of compassion among the population that keeps them from leaving the Kevins of their nations in such desperation. In our nation, where religious faith is still commonly practiced, there is not enough compassion to muster the desire to change the system, so that the sick can receive life-saving healthcare without then being killed by the bill.

Please Donate to Poor Pharmaceutical Companies

> There are three times as many pharmaceutical lobbyists on Capitol Hill than there are elected officials. How might we shift our concern from corporate profits toward affordable medications and meaningful research?

> If pharmaceutical companies can make a profit selling their medications for 60 percent less in Canada than what they charge in the United States, shouldn't we be able to get a similar deal in the United States?

> Can the profit motive drive meaningful research in new medications?

If you have an email address then you have been offered large sums of money from foreign royalty, magical male "enhancing" herbs, and a chance to save money by buying your prescription drugs through a Canadian pharmacy.

Of the three, the Canadian pharmacy stands a chance of being a legitimate offer. American made drugs are cheaper in Canada, sometimes by as much as 60 percent. Why? Because Canadian provinces cap drug prices at a level that is still profitable for the pharmaceutical companies but not as wildly profitable as in unregulated America.[5]

Why don't we do the same thing in the United States? The argument is that pharmaceutical companies need that extra profit to develop new drugs. And therein lies a major shift in American science. During the twentieth century the United States became the world leader in most areas of technology, medicine, and agriculture. We set up universities where research went hand in hand with education. University professors applied for grants from the National Science Foundation, presenting their case for why their research was relevant and how it might produce helpful new knowledge and products. Largely as a result of that research, we have been ushered into the modern era. Professors typically earn middle class salaries while their graduate students receive nothing or barely livable compensation for their long hours of work in research.

A walk through the labs of a university in Oklahoma, where I personally had reason to regularly visit, revealed a surprising amount of idle space as funding for science research had been steadily cut. We are starving our university science programs where we have some rational control over what kind of research and development is taking place while giving billions to pharmaceutical companies with no strings attached, in the hope that they will use the money to do something good. The result of this generous bargain is huge compensation for corporate executives and dividends for investors and we now have four different kinds of medication for erectile dysfunction. Meanwhile applications for university research into such things as drought-resistant wheat go unfunded.

Further, as science becomes less of a priority in our schools, the ratio of American students to foreign students in our science PhD programs continues to tilt towards foreign students. While politicians fret over illegal immigration, the real immigrant battle goes on in our universities where even a casual walk through the laboratory buildings will give you the chance to meet brilliant young African, Arab, and Asian students but not many Americans who are able to study science at an advanced level.

We find ourselves arguing over who picks our fruit, lays our bricks, or shingles our roof, while we are abdicating our role as a world leader in

5. Bihari, "Why Are Medications Cheaper to Buy in Canada?"

science. And as dismal as the Obama administration has been in science funding, what might we expect from the people who deny evolution and global climate change, i.e., the field of anti-science Republican politicians?[6]

Can We Find Common Ground on Saving Money?

> Hospitals establish elaborate policies to avoid exposure to litigation. The cost of this is passed on to the patient. How might we limit this huge expense to patients?
>
> With a single payer system operated by the Federal government, spurious lawsuits could be dismissed, drastically reducing overall medical costs. Would you be willing to give up a large portion of your right to file medical malpractice suits in exchange for more affordable healthcare?
>
> If you were eligible to use the VA Hospital for a major surgery at no cost to you, would you? If the more Spartan environment of a VA Hospital is an acceptable choice to most people, why not expand the VA to provide a low-cost option for more citizens?

A few years ago I had my first surgical encounter with our healthcare system. I survived an outpatient procedure that took less than fifteen minutes in the operating room. The bills for this procedure amounted to about $7,000.

How is it possible to rack up costs at a rate of $28,000 per hour? Had my doctor agreed to perform this simple procedure in his office, it would have cost me about $300. However, due to the slight chance of a complication, he needed to do it in the hospital. Was that to protect me or to protect him from potential liability claims? Once the decision is made to use a hospital operating room, the hospital requires that patients come in for a pre-admission meeting with anesthesiologists and other staff members to be sure that they have been given what amounts to being read your Miranda Rights prior to surgery.

Of course, my brief encounter did not amount to a real education in anesthesia, and I sure wasn't going to ask them not to bother giving me any anesthesia, so my signature on the release forms was entirely *pro forma*. Who is paying for all of this staff time made necessary by hospital lawyers

---

6. Nurse, Paul. "Stamp Out Anti-Science in US Politics."

and insurance companies to protect the hospital from lawsuits? In this case, I did, but in all cases, we do.

But consider the difference in what conservatives would call a "socialist" healthcare system such as the Veterans Health Administration. In a VA hospital, a patient can only sue after obtaining permission from the federal government. As you might imagine, permission is only granted when something egregious has happened. Hence, the cost of having obtained my surgery in a VA system would have been less than $1000.

To be clear, I liked my doctor and was generally quite satisfied with my treatment. But this cost me $5000 out of pocket, almost all of which went to pay for hospital and physician liability protection. Faced with an unavoidable surgery, I would have gladly signed release forms to get the procedure done in the most cost-effective way, but under our current system, we don't get that choice. Until we put a public option or single-payer system in place, we will continue to be forced to make huge sacrifices at the altar of insurance companies. It's not socialism; it's economic conservatism and that's where the left and right should happily meet.

Social and Scientific

7

Sexuality

". . . on analysis, humans have no substantive reason to blush for being human . . . Why is anyone embarrassed about having to do what everyone on earth does?"

On Shame and the Human Condition

Sexual mores evolved to serve the needs of a particular society but should rules for sexual behavior that served a pre-birth control, agrarian society still be in force in our day?

Sex between consenting adults is morally wrong when . . . ?

Politicians refer to the personal sex lives of political rivals to render their opponents unelectable. Should we still pay attention to this kind of *ad hominem* attack?

There was a curious television commercial, in which a young boy accusingly questions the driver of a Chevrolet Volt, an electric vehicle, about why he is stopped at a gas station. The boy deduces that the man has really stopped to use the restroom, and for some reason, the driver is embarrassed, and insists that he has not stopped to use the restroom.

My question is, "Why is anyone embarrassed about having to do what everyone on earth does?" Shame is a curiously human malady.

My counseling professor in seminary was seriously disfigured and disabled from polio. In a discussion of human sexuality, she said to us, "You look at me and assume that someone as ugly as I am would not have orgasms, but I want to assure you that you are mistaken. And I want for you to remember that in working with your counseling clients, no matter how much they may seem to be driven by shame to deny it, that they do too."

Mark Twain once observed that humans are the only species that blushes, and we are the only one that needs to. But, on analysis, humans have no substantive reason to blush for being human. We eat, sleep, defecate, and copulate just as the rest of the animal kingdom does. The only difference is that our species has developed rules, opinions, tabloid publications, and muckraking media to impose shame on other members of our species for these fundamental functions of life.

We are horribly hypocritical about it. Newt Gingrich, while married to his second wife, was allegedly having sex with the woman who would become his third wife, in a parking garage near the Capitol where he was prosecuting President Clinton for having had an extramarital affair with a woman who had done everything humanly possible to persuade the president to have sex with her. Gingrich showed no moral outrage at his own infidelity but was apoplectic about Clinton's indiscretion. This example of sexual McCarthyism is repeated throughout history, across the bounds of professions, continents, and genders.

General David Petraeus and his biographer, Colonel Paula Broadwell, had their dalliance aired in the media. It is true enough that both Petraeus and Broadwell were being unfaithful to their respective spouses, but they should have been allowed to come to terms with that infidelity within the confines of their respective families, and you and I should not have been force fed details through the barrage of virtually unavoidable media.

Predictably, once you begin to pull the thread of another person's private sin, a fabric of convoluted moral failures begins to unravel. It was discovered that the woman who first reported the affair to an FBI agent might have had inappropriate relationships of her own, even with the FBI agent who started the investigation. Please, God, save us from looking any further into how many other characters those people were salaciously entangled with!

And so, the man who was charged with the phenomenally complex job of managing our international intelligence to protect our nation from terrorist attacks (which he evidently did remarkably well) resigned from that post, though surely we never found some eunuch who is innocent of embarrassing human foibles to take his place.

If personal moral purity is the standard for this or any other position, what mortal would be qualified to hold the job?

America's Crooked Road to Same-Sex Marriage

> The June 2015 Supreme Court decision to make same-sex mar-
> riage legal in all fifty states settles the legal challenge to access to
> marriage for gay couples; where do you see the next important
> battle for the "minds and hearts" of those who have held onto
> prejudices against same-sex couples?
>
> Would you take any personal risks in employment, family, or
> friendship relationships in defense of the rights of same-sex
> couples?
>
> Why do you believe America was so late in legalizing same-sex mar-
> riage when so many less developed nations had already done so?

I moved to America's heartland in the summer of 1991 to be the pastor of a
large denominational church. At my first board meeting, I was challenged
by an angry church member who asked, "What are you going to do about
the queers?" I had no idea how big a part of the next two decades of my life
would be consumed with trying to answer that question, nor how much my
answers were going to cost me personally and professionally.

Missouri was the first state in the nation to pass a state constitutional
amendment banning same-sex marriage. I said in a newspaper column at
that time, in 2004, that we would soon be as ashamed of that fact as we are
now ashamed of our history of racial segregation. "Soon," was an exces-
sively optimistic prediction. In fact, this constitutional black eye was still
on the books when the Supreme Court rendered all such state laws moot.

In the summer of 2004, I held a press conference to articulate religious
objections to this discriminatory amendment. I invited clergy from all over
the city to join me in that press conference. A rabbi and a couple of retired
members of Christian clergy did join me, but no other pastors of Christian
congregations risked an appearance. I did, however, receive a number of
phone calls from pastors who said that they would like to be there but they
were afraid of being fired. "I have a family to provide for, and I cannot risk
losing my job," one sad pastor said.

I replied, "If we all stood up for justice at the same time, they couldn't
fire all of us. They can only pick us off one at a time if the majority remains
in the shadows."

At the time, it appeared that the religion-inspired prejudice against our gay sisters and brothers was a dying patient for whom the marriage amendment was only a last gasp.

Vanderbilt Divinity School, where I had earned both my master's and doctoral degrees, was not only the first Divinity School in the country to have a female dean, but we discovered in my first year there, she was also the first lesbian dean. Though I had a pretty typical rural Kentucky prejudice about homosexuality when I went to grad school, most of that had been educated out of me by the time my diplomas were hung on the wall over my desk in Springfield, Missouri.

However, I had never tried to persuade anyone else that, as I replied in that board meeting, "there is no reason to believe that God hates gay people." My answer had to get a lot better than that, as I have been called upon in multiple church meetings, Bible studies, college classrooms, and denominational meetings to explain how I am a Christian pastor and biblical scholar who does not believe that it is wrong, either from a social ethics perspective or a theological perspective, to be in a same-sex relationship.

Slowly, painfully, and with many fractured friendships and lost parishioners, religious leaders are coming around to acknowledging that whatever has fueled their anti-gay sentiments, it has nothing to do with a religion that is inherently defined by love and compassion. People can change, though typically they don't change much, and they don't change very fast.

While traveling in rural Nicaragua, way up a dirt road in one of the most isolated villages in this traditionally Catholic, machismo-driven nation, I saw a poster on the community center wall advocating for safe sex in the gay community. I was stunned to see such openness in an area I have been visiting for the past decade, where, it seemed to me, homosexuality would have been dangerous even to mention.

In a conversation later that night with area residents, a young man, ironically named "Jesus," told me that he is gay, and he described the changing world of Nicaragua, in which religious prejudices are quickly losing their power. The national government had recently passed legislation to protect women from violence and to create an education campaign in their schools against bullying.

As an armchair sociologist, I am still at a complete loss for how a largely uneducated and untraveled population could embrace such a dramatic evolution of awareness years before the Supreme Court of the United States forced the issue here. Still, if a population deeply steeped in religious bias can do this with few of the advantages of enlightenment we have from media, travel, and higher education, then maybe one day we will too.

The Supreme Court has removed legal hurdles to make same-sex marriage legal in all fifty states. We have won the legal battle, but the fight for the hearts and minds of religious people remains.

Who Should Be on the Sex Offenders List?

> Should those found guilty of possessing child pornography be on the same sex offender list with people who have been found guilty of abducting and raping children?
>
> Should people (especially adolescents) who are found guilty of misdemeanor offenses such as indecent exposure, be able to eventually get their names off the sex offender list?
>
> Since sex offenders typically find it nearly impossible to find housing or employment, what should we do with sex offenders? Is there a way to get them back into a productive role in society?
>
> If it benefits the public to have a list of sex offenders, should we also have lists for other kinds of offenses such as embezzlement or burglary?
>
> Is being on the sex offender list intended to be helpful information for the community, or is it simply a part of the punishment?

The symbol most often seen on law offices and courthouses is an image of a set of balanced scales. What we want from our penal system is justice—balanced justice—in which we can reliably believe that the punishment fits the crime. Everyone knows that there is a difference between murder and littering. In fact, we discern several different degrees of murder: involuntary manslaughter, premeditated murder, and crimes of passion. We understand that there is a huge moral difference between accidentally killing someone in a vehicular homicide and going into a former place of employment with automatic weapons and killing everyone you can. We expect our government, our judges, and our penal system to deliver punishment that fits the crime. Not too little and not too much.

I would like to call for a moment of sane reflection on balanced justice when it comes to being permanently included on a list of sex offenders. Like most people, I wouldn't waste much breath in defending anyone who had sexually molested children, or who had committed forced sodomy or rape. In fact, when I have moved into a neighborhood, because I have a daughter, I have always consulted the sex offenders' registry to see if I have any neighbors about whom I should be concerned.

The only legitimate reason to have such a list is to warn residents about the presence of criminals who might pose a threat. However, what we find on the list is not just child molesters and rapists. Here are some examples of persons you might find listed in your area: One is a young mother who recently escaped from a violent marriage to a man who molested her children. She did not report her ex-husband's abuse, because he had threatened to kill her. Maybe she should have reported him, but she was young and terrified. Even though she was also a victim of her husband's violence, she was charged as an accomplice to the child molestation, and now will be forced to register as a sex offender for the rest of her life.

Another might be a middle-aged man who, twenty years ago, was having a cookout in a public park with some college buddies. He drank too much beer and decided to relieve himself behind a tree in the park. A family with children saw him urinating in public, and called the police. He was convicted of indecent exposure and will now be on the sex offender list for the rest of his life.

The list, which was created to help parents feel safer, has become yet another club with which the justice system can unevenly and irrationally beat down people who otherwise might have gotten their lives straightened out and become healthy and productive members of society.

Keep the list, but please make sure that only genuine sex offenders are on it.

Time to Start Talking About the "T" in LGBT

It turns out that gender identity is more complicated than the traditional "Male or Female" boxes we have been checking on forms our entire lives. How does adjusting our thinking to include trans and gender-fluid individuals affect our social norms?

When a high profile person such as the former Olympic champion, Bruce Jenner, begins to publicly talk about his or her gender transformation, does the media create healthy and educational conversations on the topic, or does it tend to turn make the issue into a carnival show?

> When people are forced to live as the gender they were assigned
> at birth, but they feel that they are the other gender, how do you
> think that affects their marriage and family relationships? How do
> they cope?

Though the world has gone through a virtual sea change of opinion regarding gay and lesbian rights, same-sex marriage and even the religious prejudice regarding same-sex relationships, the "T" in LGBT is still an awkward topic for many. A lot of the problem in setting aside fears and prejudice of the transgender community is rooted in the relatively smaller numbers of people who, by their DNA, are one gender, but in their mind feel strongly that they are the other. Much of the progress in dispelling the prejudice against gays and lesbians has come from the fact that more and more people have come out of the closet, and most of us in the heterosexual majority have realized that a member of our own family or a close friend is gay.

As we have witnessed in the too-much-talked-about "Duck Dynasty" star's insensitivity, anti-gay prejudice is now no more acceptable than is old-school racism. We understand that sexual orientation is a matter of birth, and we would no more ask our gay friend to live as a straight person than we who are straight would accept being forced into same-sex relationships.

What is more difficult for many in the straight and gay communities to appreciate is that, for some people, gender identity is less clear, and may be a very painful and deeply personal journey of discovery.

It is difficult to say what percentage of the population we are talking about, though some of the transgender community come from intersexed births. Many people are surprised to discover that children who are born with both male and female sex organs are not that rare, statistically occurring in one of every 1,500 births. Gender uncertainty or irregularity is even more common. Some biblical scholars have speculated that it was just such a personal anomaly that accounted for the Apostle Paul's rather adamant views regarding marriage and sexual conduct.

When my Mexican friend asks me to join him at his favorite restaurant, he enjoys the menudo soup. I don't mind him eating it, but the thought of eating a cow's stomach lining is repulsive to me — and I've eaten camel burger in Egypt, guinea pig in Ecuador, and iguana in Nicaragua! Anyone who has ever eaten an American hot dog should not feel superior to any other culture's culinary delights. A personal feeling of revulsion at anything that is foreign to us or for which we have no similar desire does not amount to a logical reason to be prejudiced. But unlike tastes in food, sexual orientation is not learned or chosen from a menu. It goes to the deepest part of who a person is. All that the transgender community is asking for is to be allowed to be who they are, to live comfortably inside their own skin.

For a member of the transgender community, the journey to becoming externally the person he or she feels she or he is internally is difficult enough without the majority population (both gay and straight) adding prejudice and misinformed demands to the process. The public has finally accepted the fact that you cannot "catch" gay by being around gay people. Now people need to get over the fear that sharing a public restroom with someone who is changing genders is going to hurt them in any way.

Matters of Law and Matters of the Heart

> If you once were opposed to same-sex marriage and feel differently now, can you remember what changed your views?
>
> If you belong to a church that has become open and affirming, can you describe the journey from prejudice to equality?
>
> If you have changed your views on homosexuality over the past few years, did the change come because you discovered that someone you cared about was gay, or did a class, Bible study, or ideological argument play the largest role in that transformation?

I stood with a young couple as they repeated their marriage vows in the presence of God and all the eager witnesses that could crowd into the living room of a bed and breakfast. One was a physician who would later become a decorated officer in the Iraq War; the other was a research scientist. We held their wedding in the mid-1990s in Eureka Springs, an Arkansas mountain retreat, because they were both women and they were not welcome to be married in the church they attended and financially supported. As the pastor of that church, I needed to be a hundred miles away from my congregation's board members who surely would have, in a fit of Christian love, fired me for conducting this service.

Over the next several years, I pushed the envelope, serving as celebrant in same-sex weddings in local Chinese restaurants and private homes while my church employers continued to say, "Not here." Prejudice dies slowly and painfully. There were several mile markers in that church's journey as it changed. Eventually, gay couples were photographed together in the church directory. A gay liturgist mentioned his partner in a Sunday service, and a gay poet read a love poem at a Valentine's dinner.

The last time the board officially voted to prevent me from performing a same-sex wedding in the church, one board member raised his hand and asked, "When a gay person puts a check in the offering plate, do we cash that check?" The hypocrisy was revealed, but it was still five more years before the policy changed. A much-loved member of the church staff stayed in the closet for fifteen years to protect himself from the righteous Christian love of the congregation that surely would have publicly humiliated him while making him unemployed.

Slowly, as many of the most anti-gay churchgoers either softened or went to other churches, I was eventually allowed to perform a same-sex union in the sanctuary. Still, there was threatening anonymous mail and even one letter signed by an attorney in the church who claimed that what I was doing was illegal and that I would be going to jail. Illegally asking God's blessing on a love relationship became a prejudice consigned to history, thanks to the Supreme Court of the United States (SCOTUS) when it finally handed down a decision that settled the matter.

Still, the battle is not over. Though the SCOTUS can make decisions regarding law, it cannot overrule personal prejudice. The federal government will no longer discriminate, but many individuals still feel the same disdain and I wonder how many churches would still fire their pastor for asking for God's blessing on a committed love relationship? In spite of it all, I suspect that within a decade, nearly everyone will vociferously deny having ever expressed a negative feeling against same-sex marriage.

Science Doesn't Care What You Believe

Science corrects itself in the presence of new information that contradicts previous beliefs. Can religions do the same thing?

For years, the debate about sexual orientation revolved around whether it was a matter of choice or a matter of inherent nature. We are now discovering that the "gay or straight" dichotomy doesn't cover the reality of many more subtle and fluid aspects of human sexuality. Can you be flexible enough to keep a close friendship with someone who is gender-fluid?

Should any religious values be a part of the legal code, even if the religion is held by a supermajority of the citizens?

Michael Dowd, the author of *Thank God for Evolution,* and his wife, Connie, a science journalist, have made it their life's work to travel, write, and teach about the inevitable connection between spirituality and science. He sometimes makes me a bit uncomfortable in his dismissal of ancient religious texts in favor of "scientific evidence as our new scripture." My discomfort comes from feeling like a dinosaur, with an awful lot of education in those ancient texts, yet I bow to the inevitable truth that rational evidence will take the place of all *a priori* truths.

Where religion sets itself up in opposition to science, religion is writing its own epitaph. As I have watched the debate between pastors on the opinion page of my local newspaper regarding matters of sexual orientation, the words of Shakespeare's Macbeth keep coming to mind, because the debate seems to me to be, "full of sound and fury, signifying nothing."

Some people are gay. Some people are straight. Those are just the facts and religious beliefs cannot change that reality. Several years ago, in a church I was serving, I was asked to hold a vote on whether to become officially "open and affirming." My response was, "What would it mean if the board voted against that resolution? Would our gay members suddenly stop being gay because they didn't have board approval?" A church can no more vote on sexual orientation than it can vote on gravity. Churches that hope to have a future must deal with reality, not superstition.

I am deeply sorry for the discrimination that same-sex couples have suffered at the hands of conservative Christians, but when literalist Christians have diminished in size to match the "Flat Earth Society" there will still be gay people and straight people. Still, as I have pointed out in conversation with Michael Dowd, a recent Gallop Poll showed that 51 percent of Southerners and 49 percent of people in the Midwest still believe that God created humans in their present form within the last 10,000 years. The percentages on the east and west coasts are somewhat less discouraging, but the numbers across the United States call into doubt the efficacy of our science teachers. It may be a tribute to conservative churches that they can restrain the beneficial effects of a century of science education in half of the population, but this denial of reality cannot last much longer.

It doesn't matter if you put ten thousand people in a giant "Six Flags Over Jesus" church, beat drums, shout, dance, speak in tongues, listen to impassioned and tearful sermons, and come away absolutely convinced that the earth is flat, because, dear readers, the earth is not flat. You can put a million people in a church and wave ancient texts over their heads that were written by people of faith who did not know where the sun goes at night, but who still told you that homosexuality is a sin, and it still doesn't change anything. Some folks are straight and some are gay.

Many gay people have been manipulated by religious fear and guilt into trying to live in straight relationships. That unnatural circumstance has led to miserable marriages, spouse abuse, alcoholism, and suicide but it never changed one gay person into being straight, any more than the Flat Earth Society has managed to change the shape of the planet. In my estimation, the best religion deals with what is true, and not what is clearly false.

Prejudice's Chicken-Or-Egg Dilemma

> Do conservative churches teach people to have prejudice against gays and lesbians or do prejudiced people just seek out churches that affirm their pre-existent prejudices?

> Are you able to see the difference between finding something to be viscerally repulsive to you and being morally wrong?

> Do you believe that churches that hold onto negative feelings about gays and lesbians will continue to exist for the next twenty years?

When I roamed the streets of Paris, I was in awe of the architecture, the art museums, and the history of France but when I stopped in a restaurant to sample the famous fare, what I kept encountering were entrees taken from the parts of cows I would generally consider to be reserved for dog food. What I saw listed on the menus could have hardly been more repulsive to me if the offering had come straight out of a cookbook written by Hannibal Lecter.

But does the fact that much of what French chefs consider to be tasty is offensive to me make their culinary arts sinful? Of course not! Granted, I ate a lot of fried potatoes on that trip, but I was not forced to order a plate of intestines any more than the people sitting around me with smug looks on their faces were forced to join me in my purely American penchant for dipping my fries into catsup. Just asking a waiter for a bottle of catsup made them look like I had suggested something obscene, but there was usually a dusty bottle in the back reserved for uncouth American tourists.

People are quite diverse. And far from being a bad thing, that diversity is often what makes us want to travel great distances to see and to experience different cultures. I had neither a desire to become a French citizen, nor to become a citizen of any of the other nations I have visited (ok, maybe Italy . . . or Greece) because I am American by birth and by choice, but I have no need to say that everyone on earth should be American, nor do I feel that someone is wrong for being German, English, Greek, or Egyptian.

Why, then, are heterosexuals so threatened by homosexuals that they will line up by the thousands to buy really bad fried chicken as soon as they learn that the owner of the fast food chain contributes millions of dollars to promote the execution of gay people in Africa and their deportation from America?[1] I understand that gay sexual conduct is distasteful to many people, and the obvious solution to that is to not have gay sex. There are, after all, other choices on the menu.

After seeing the lines forming at Chick-Fil-A near my home, I realized how very vital it is for our city council to add sexual orientation to our non-discrimination policies. It is hard to believe that this is politically controversial in the twenty-first century but the display of homophobic prejudice masquerading as either religious fervor or advocacy of free speech makes it evident that it is not safe to be gay in many parts of this land of the free.

And to my Christian sisters and brothers who continue to point to the condemnation of homosexuality in Romans chapter 1, please let me point out to you that in that list of sins, Paul includes such things as gossip, envy, and talking back to your parents, and in the first verse of chapter 2, concludes, "Therefore you have no excuse, whoever you are, when you judge others; for in passing judgment on another you condemn yourself, because you, the judge, are doing the very same things."

Be honest with yourself. Your prejudice never had anything to do with either religion or free speech, and it can't really be about the fried chicken, especially when there is a Popeye's in town. *Bon Appétit!*

Majoring in Minors and Minoring in Majors

If the corporate news media is only giving us what the public wants, why do we continue to want to know so much about the bedroom antics of politicians?

1. Badash, "Chick-Fil-A 5 Reasons It Isn't What You Think It Is."

Repeating gossip is morally reprehensible, but the sin requires a willing listener. Are you as careful about refusing to listen to gossip as you are about not repeating it?

The news media often fails to report on matters of grave public importance, in favor of reports on fashion, sexual gossip, and the legal problems of musicians, actors, and athletes. Have you ever written to your favorite news outlet to object to this dumbing down of the news?

Years ago the comedian, Dennis Miller, said that anyone who subscribed to the gossip tabloids should be added to a mandatory sterilization list. He reasoned that anyone who thought that he or she needed this "useful information" certainly shouldn't be allowed to reproduce. Twenty-five years later, speculating about the sex lives of famous people has become primary content in broadcast news outlets.

News about the Arab Spring in Yemen and the battle to end Qaddafi's reign in Libya was ignored in favor of conversation about underwear photos texted by Congressman Anthony Weiner (insert sophomoric snicker here). And in a true bi-partisan spirit, the media likes to add sizzle to reports on both parties. No report on the 2012 presidential campaign of Newt Gingrich was complete without some reference to the fact that, while he prosecuted impeachment charges against President Clinton for the Lewinski affair, Gingrich was cheating on his wife by having sex in his car with a staffer who later became his third wife.

In a perfect world, no one would ever cheat on his or her spouse, and professionals and politicians would never take advantage of a client, patient, student, or staffer. We do not, however, live in that world. Evolutionary forces armed with modern technology make it too easy for personal weaknesses to be moved from the private universe, where they belong, onto the TV screens of an ever more gossip-hungry viewing public. There needs to be a clear distinction between sex crimes and purely personal moral indiscretions. Sex between consenting adults is their business and not ours. Marital infidelity is a matter to be dealt with privately without the public debate on whether Maria Shriver should have divorced "The" Arnold, or speculating about what Hillary actually said to Bill about Monica in their White House bedroom.

We need to focus attention on whether politicians and professionals are doing their jobs, and keep our noses out of their personal lives. Gingrich's personal life was disgusting, but he was right to criticize Senator

Paul Ryan's budget plan, and that's the sort of thing that should be discussed in a presidential election year. Weiner showed courage in Congress about important issues often ignored by other legislators. That he is a perfectly horrible excuse for a husband is not particularly relevant, but the brouhaha around his multi-media dalliances cost Congress an important voice for social justice. Good government depends on mature voters outgrowing gossip.

I am not inclined to believe that all of the bad-boy sex reporting is conscious manipulation of the voters by the media to keep us from talking about how the military budget has more than doubled in the US over the past decade while it has gone down in the budgets of our NATO partners. I don't think that it is a conspiracy on the part of insurance and pharmaceutical companies to keep the public from talking about how they are creating the healthcare crisis. I'm afraid the problem is the dumbing down of viewer tastes, and that can only change when we stop listening to this childish nonsense and begin to demand real journalism.

8

Race, Prejudice, Justice

As Gandhi said, "At first they will ignore us. Then they will make fun of us. Then they will fight us. Then we will win."

Civil Rights Demonstrations in the 21st Century

Do you believe that the June 2015 murder of nine members of the Mother Emanuel AME Church in Charleston, SC will be a significant mile marker in the American willingness to passively accept racism in our culture?

The South Carolina legislature, by a nearly unanimous vote, decided to remove the Confederate flag from the capitol grounds in Columbia. Will that event be the starting point of substantive change in the attitudes of southern whites toward their black neighbors or is that vote the finish line of what they intend to do at this time?

Which division do you believe is the more significant aspect of the divide between blacks and whites in America: racial prejudice or economic class prejudice?

We have now marked the fiftieth anniversary of a momentous event in the Civil Rights movement when four black young men went into the Woolworth in Greensboro, North Carolina and took seats at the lunch counter. They then waited to be arrested for sitting in the "whites only" eatery. Not wanting to create a media event, the college students in that act of civil disobedience were not arrested. They were allowed to sit there, without being served, until the store closed. Not to be defeated in their defiance of the Jim

Crow laws, the young men returned to the lunch counter, every day, and sat there without being served, day after day, for six months until, at last, the lunch counter was integrated.

I wonder where that resolve is in our day? We have sat back and watched as our government has failed to break down the apartheid system in America where the tax dollars of every citizen are used to fund a healthcare system that only opened its doors to about 80 percent of the population, and many of those leave the hospital to find themselves being forced into bankruptcy. We have watched as our national resources have been used to bail out our country's banks and then, when the people who caused the banking crisis reward themselves with billions of tax dollars in personal bonuses, the media and the public have stood idly by.

It wasn't just Jesus and the Apostles who were arrested, beaten, and sometimes executed for their civil disobedience. We cannot forget that the very people we now teach our children to admire: Gandhi, Martin Luther King Jr., Dorothy Day, Dietrich Bonhoeffer, Nelson Mandela, and Archbishop Oscar Romero, all suffered arrests and beatings, and in some cases, martyrdom, in the process of defying unjust circumstances.

If we admire Gandhi's salt march and Martin Luther King's bus boycott, why are we not able to see that something of their courage and public demonstration will be required of us to actually change the oligarchic system of oppressive government we now have? What would a peaceful civil demonstration look like in our day?

Could a few dozen concerned citizens block access to a local hospital? It would be considered a crime, even though the insurance companies and hospitals refusing to treat millions of sick Americans is not currently viewed as a crime. What if a group were to surround a local bank with crime scene tape and refuse to allow anyone to enter the bank for a day? You would get arrested though you probably wouldn't be beaten or crucified.

Our elected officials are doing the bidding of their political donors. A lot of the electorate has even been recruited into "don't you dare give us healthcare" tea parties with a wink and a "you betcha" from an aging cheerleader.

Now that the former Woolworth in Greensboro has opened as a museum, one is forced to wonder if it is actually just a memorial to the time when Americans cared enough to act and were smart enough to know that they do not have to accept second-class citizenship.

Civil Disobedience and the Payday Loan Business

Have you ever participated in a protest or a demonstration? Would you do so again?

What makes a demonstration successful?

Should churches be involved in public protests for social justice causes?

Somewhat shaken by a small turnout at a demonstration, I am reminded of the closing lines of Percy Bysshe Shelley's poem that he wrote following the Peterloo Massacre, *The Masque of Anarchy*, in which he advocated for non-violent resistance:

"Rise like Lions after slumber
In unvanquishable number-
Shake your chains to earth like dew
Which in sleep had fallen on you
Ye are many-they are few."[1]

Returning from what would typically be called a "successful" protest in front of one of our city's more egregiously offensive payday loan businesses, I have pondered why so few people show up at such events, especially considering the tens of thousands of people victimized by predatory lenders. A small protest of this sort rarely merits more than twenty seconds of coverage on TV and a brief story in print media. If we were lucky, we might provoke one of the radio talk shows into spending five or six minutes droning on about how we are un-American and anti-business because we believe that collecting 1900 percent interest on a loan is really evil.

What is disheartening to me is that almost every public demonstration is comprised of a dozen or so folks from the same pool of a couple of dozen people. The majority of the people at any such event are either retired or unemployed, and most of them are my personal friends or members of my small congregation. Notices for meetings such as the one mentioned above have gone to as many as five thousand people on various activist lists, but the turnout is less than one-fourth of one percent of the people in our area who have identified themselves as progressive thinkers.

1. Wikipedia, "The Masque of Anarchy."

Psychologically speaking, anger is more motivating than compassion, but progressives get angry too. We get angry about working to elect a Democratic president, senate, and congress, only to watch them do the same things as their Republican predecessors, but our anger does not appear to result in action the way conservative anger can bring out thousands of people just to hear a speech from an Alaskan empty vessel.

How do we persuade progressives to stand up from their computer keyboards and actually show up to make their beliefs known, and show their elected representatives that they will not accept being treated like mindless door-knocking, voter-registering, cash cows? The reason why the Democratic Party believes that they can count on our votes is because progressives do not gather en masse.

There is a Coffee Party that has tried to be the progressive answer to the Tea Party but unless you put your name on their mailing list, you don't hear much about them. There are advocacy groups for workers, for the LGBT community, for reproductive rights, for racial minorities, and for immigrants, but there isn't enough collaboration to get the numbers we saw during the Civil Rights movement or the Vietnam War protests that were so successful in effecting change.

Liberals resist being organized. We tend to be intolerant of those who do not agree with us 100 percent of the time. We drop out of organizations on a whim over the most venial of offenses. And therefore, we remain only marginally effective in all of our causes. The Will McAvoy character in *The Newsroom* poses the challenge colorfully: If liberals are so f****** smart, how come they lose so goddamn always?

My belief is that we will continue to lose nearly always until we become sufficiently committed to one another to come out for one another's causes and start standing together in numbers the public cannot ignore. Blacks need to support labor issues. Men need to support Planned Parenthood. Whites need to support Black Lives Matter. Progressives need to show up to support movements that may not be your most important focus because we need to be able to care about more than one thing at a time!

Nazis and Evangelicals

> Does prejudice that is motivated by religious belief deserve more tolerance than the same prejudice motivated by either political or personal motivations?

Can a reasonable expectation of violence at a protest justify using the police to prevent the protest? When does "free speech" become "terroristic threatening?"

When do persons of conscience decide to forego personal safety to place themselves physically in harm's way to protect the rights of minorities?

"Time," Woody Allen observed, "is nature's way of keeping everything from happening all at once." Still, sometimes the things that happen simultaneously can seem to make time stand still by the weight of sheer irony. The day I read in my local newspaper that our city's Human Rights Commission was being cut from the city's budget, I was also handed a notice published by the local neo-Nazi group, the National Socialist Movement, announcing their intentions to disrupt the coming weekend's Pride Fest.

The plight of the gay community in my Midwestern town has certainly improved over the past decade, but we are a long way from being the kind of city that is so free of racial, gender and sexual prejudice that we can close down our Human Rights Commission. In the absence of a city-funded office to advocate for the targets of discrimination and hate crimes, persons of conscience must become increasingly willing to publicly and visibly stand up in defense of the rights of minorities in Springfield.

In 2001, a local black man was stabbed by neo-Nazi skinheads in a Denny's restaurant, ostensibly because he was sitting with his white girlfriend. The perpetrators of these hate crimes can be difficult to apprehend when they are acting in a group. It took nearly three years to find and charge those responsible for the knife attack on Maurice Wilson. We are fortunate that the attackers were found and identified at all because these gangs tend to move their members around the country to avoid detection and apprehension. One flabby, tattooed, bald guy, with bad teeth looks a lot like other dentally challenged, heavily tattooed, hairless, unemployed, corpulent men.

I had been invited to speak at the Pride Fest, and was weighing that invitation against an invitation to go to a friend's lake house. The thought of a gang of thugs in black uniforms decorated with red swastikas attempting to disrupt the Pride Fest sealed my decision. The stated goal of this little gang of terrorists was to "let the homosexuals know that they are not welcome in our town and that we will not tolerate their 'celebration.'"

As I have often pointed out to my New Testament students, "The only thing Jesus was intolerant of was intolerance." The Nazis went to the event to try to terrorize gays into either leaving town or going back into the "closet." These are times when straight people need to make the plight of their gay neighbors their own, taking a stand with the gay community to protect their right to be who they are, and to celebrate their culture, their love relationships, and their lives, and to do so without fear of judgment, intimidation, or violence.

As our culture becomes more diverse, and more churches and businesses become adamantly open and affirming, all of our communities become more interesting and enjoyable places to live. Gays are always welcome. Intolerance, however, is on its way out.

When I took the stage to speak to the gathered crowd, the scene before me looked like the rings of Dante's Inferno. From the elevation of the stage, I could look over the heads of my hometown's out and proud gay community to the closest ring just outside of the event's fenced area. There, on the sidewalks were angry looking people carrying very large Bibles and holding signs with messages of condemnation for the families and children who were trying to enjoy the music, food, and displays of the festival. The next circle I could see, beyond the ring of witnessing Evangelicals, was the small band of neo-Nazis whom police kept mostly across the street.

The Nazis carried signs that read "Thank God for HIV," and through a megaphone they shouted "death to gays." The Fascist-wannabes form one layer of disgustingly prejudiced society, but when I looked at the larger number of Bible-carrying critics, I was forced to wonder how much difference there really is between someone shouting that they hope the homosexuals die of AIDS and the ones who repeatedly shouted their warnings that homosexuals would burn in hell forever . . . Or even, which one is more frighteningly insane?

The Nazis interviewed on TV that weekend simply could not understand why they were being so discriminated against, and yet they feel entirely justified in cheering for a deadly disease to strike the families gathered at the Pride Fest. The evangelicals would tell you that they are trying to save souls from hell as they continue to teach and promote the condemnation of the gay community. For centuries, this has resulted in making homosexuals the targets of hate crimes, discrimination in the workplace, divisions within families, and even refusal of healthcare. With a loving religion like that, who needs Nazis?

How Many Innocents Are You Willing to Kill?

Since more than 150 people on death row have been found to be innocent since the death penalty was reinstated in 1973, how confident should we be in the justice system's ability to be sufficiently certain of anyone's guilt to merit execution?[2]

Persons of color make up a disproportionate percentage of the prisoners on death row. When you consider the role of race in the frequency of death sentences, it seems clear that when a black man kills a white man, the chances of execution go up dramatically when compared to any other instance of violent crime. How can we tolerate such a sharp racial divide when it is literally a matter of life and death?[3]

Though it is impossible to say what would have happened if the laws were different, criminologists tend to agree that capital punishment is not successful as a deterrent to homicide. Is revenge a sufficient reason for a state to execute a prisoner?[4]

It is estimated to cost as much as ten times as much to execute a prisoner as it costs to keep the same prisoner incarcerated for life. If that is true, what is our motivation for execution?

In the ancient biblical account of the destruction of the infamous cities of Sodom and Gomorrah, the patriarch tried to persuade the Almighty not to kill the innocent with the guilty. He asked God, "Will you indeed sweep away the righteous with the wicked?" So begins the bargaining session with the anthropomorphic God of Genesis. God offers to stay the execution of the inhabitants of the condemned cities if Abraham can find fifty innocent people. The patriarch, well aware that righteousness was in scarce supply, negotiated until the number needed to stop the destruction was lowered to twenty, and finally to only ten righteous people. Sadly, the story doesn't end well, because the patriarch couldn't even come up with ten who could be used to spare the cities, but you have to applaud Abraham's effort.

I would like to take up Abraham's argument once again: What if we could show that some of the people on death row are not actually guilty

2. Death Penalty Information Center, "Innocence List."

3. ACLU, "Race and the Death Penalty."

4. Death Penalty Information Center, "Facts about Deterrence and the Death Penalty."

of the crimes with which they are charged? If, in fact, several states have executed people who were not guilty—then aren't those states guilty of murder? What if we could show that fifty of the people on death row are not guilty, would that be enough to prove that we shouldn't be sufficiently confident in our justice system to execute anyone? What if we would find seventy-five or one hundred innocent people? Or what if the number is over one hundred-fifty?—because that's how many people on death row have been found to be innocent since capital punishment became legal again in 1973.

Many persons of conscience across the country are calling for a moratorium on executions until a thorough review can be done of every case. I add my name to the list of persons seeking this moratorium, because I am aware that the justice system is presently tilted unjustly towards the rich. Most of those who find themselves facing execution could not afford to hire their own legal counsel, and many find themselves being placed on death row, not because of their guilt, but because they are too poor to mount an adequate defense.

While I recognize that we still are far from agreement as to whether or not the state has the right to execute a prisoner, we should all adamantly refuse to kill the innocent with the guilty.

Badges and Brains

> Should a municipal government be able to refuse to hire a candidate for a police force because the applicant has an above-average IQ?

> Should there be a minimum IQ for certain public service positions, or even to hold elected office?

> Do you believe that there could be a connection between recent incidents of racial prejudice in several police shootings of unarmed victims and the practice of hiring only average-intelligence police candidates?

Robert Jordan, a forty-nine year old college graduate, applied to be a member of the police force in New London, NY, but he was not hired because of the score on his IQ test. Though his score was the equivalent of an IQ of 121, just above-average, Jordan was deemed to be too smart. He sued the city, and the city successfully defended its hiring policy in court, and again on appeal, arguing that a person with above-average intelligence would get bored in police work and would not last long on the force, wasting expensive training resources. Of course, that excuse seems much less plausible than assuming that the city has a preference for hiring employees who are more likely to be compliant, but I can be kind of cynical about excuses for discrimination, especially in light of the recent spate of stories about apparent prejudice among the police.

Jordan's case raises a number of questions about policing in the United States. Since the leadership on police forces inevitably rises from the ranks of the force, we can assume that we have no police chiefs with above-average intelligence? Shouldn't we demand more?

How could so many obviously C and D grade minds have arrived in so many important positions of leadership? So, we come back to the case of Robert Jordan. If you find yourself in a situation where you call the police to send officers carrying lethal weapons, would you like those officers to be of above-average intelligence? If you should have to undergo serious surgery, do you want the surgeon who graduated at the bottom of the class, or at the top of the class? This is not a matter of being elitist; this is a matter of competence.

I'm not suggesting that all police recruits should be of above-average IQ. Surely a case could be made for the benefits of a mix of people with average and above-average IQ scores, but can't we see that excluding those who are more intellectually gifted from these forms of public service is not in our best interests? Look what excluding gifted people has done for us in congress!

Domestic Abuse

> Have you ever known a victim of domestic abuse? What did you do to intervene?
>
> In almost every case, domestic abusers grew up in abusive homes. What do you think works best to break that cycle?
>
> Do you believe that it is possible for a marriage to become healthy again after an incident of physical violence between spouses?

I see battered women every week. The bruised faces, broken arms and, in one case, a cut-throat (yes, she survived and reconciled to her abuser when he got out of jail) are by-products of the stress of extreme poverty, homelessness, and addiction, along with frequently untreated mental illness. And though it doesn't happen often, I have also been called by the live in-maid of parishioners, awakened by the violent fighting of her employers. Like the woman who took back the abuser who cut her throat, this wife, an educated, professional woman, would look at me in their living room and say, "My husband is perfect."

The small city where I live has fewer than two hundred thousand citizens. The facility that houses victims of spouse abuse has just over one hundred beds. The director of this facility has told me that if he had five hundred beds, he could keep them filled with our present level of demand. And that is for those who do want to leave their abuser. On average, a woman will reconcile with her abuser seven to eight times before finally getting healthy enough to get out of the relationship and stay out of it. With the right kind of support, victims can cut that cycle of abuse, and more quickly move into a healthier way of living.

Still, one of the biggest problems at all domestic abuse shelters is the common habit of victims calling their abuser and asking him to come visit. Signs on the walls of transitional housing units for those who have moved out of the shelter and are preparing for an apartment of their own remind residents that they cannot have "guests" in the rooms because, most often, the guest is the abuser.

There may be a plethora of reasons for the high rate of domestic violence in the small city where I live, but at least one obvious factor is that we just don't provide enough resources to address the problem effectively. Two hundred miles up the road from us, in Kansas City's shelter program, Rose Brooks spends twice as much per victim cared for, and much of that money is spent in community education. The result has been that even in this urban area, the rate of both child and spouse abuse is less than half of what it is here in the Ozarks.

Prevention is obviously preferable to treatment. As the modern proverb goes, it doesn't make sense to keep bandaging people up at the bottom of the cliff without ever climbing to the top, to stop whoever is throwing them off in the first place. We need to get abuse case workers into our schools, by middle school, to teach young women how to avoid being victimized, and to teach young men how to avoid the controlling behaviors that lead to violence.

This is a perennial problem, but it is not one that defies treatment. If only our citizens can overcome their indifference, there are lots of ways to help.

Urban Racism

> Why was taking Palestinian land to form a Jewish homeland accept-able, but giving North America back to Native Americans is not?

> The Sunni-Shia divide in Islam is now entering its fifteenth cen-tury. What could be done to resolve the violent conflicts between these two divisions of Islam?

> Though many prejudices are misrepresentations of an ethnic group, some are rooted in real experience or cultural differences. How do we move our multi-cultural nation from a point of fear and prejudice to a sincere celebration of cultural diversity?

"Those wise guys don't care about nobody," my cab driver said as he pointed toward two men working off of the back of a delivery truck carelessly parked so that it blocked traffic in the crowded Brooklyn street. That was where my impromptu and unwanted education in urban racism began. Once irritated by one long and unnecessary delay, my driver felt compelled to instruct his Midwestern passenger on the moral failings of each of the ethnic groups we passed on the hour long drive from LaGuardia to the lower Manhattan site where I would officiate at a friend's wedding.

Pointing at two young Hasidic Jews, my driver informed me, "They have all the money and they keep it, that's why everyone else is so poor and has such a hard life." According to my driver, all of the Latino women in New York City are popping out babies, all Muslims are up to some insidious plot, and all black men are just trying to park their trucks in a way to keep him from being able to make a decent living.

In an attempt to change the subject, I commented on his obvious ac-cent and told him how much I had enjoyed the time I had spent touring his European country. "Well you wouldn't like it anymore," he said, "people are immigrating from everywhere, just jumping off the ships and walking onto shore and they never leave!" I didn't point out the phenomenal hypocrisy of his feelings about immigrants while being an immigrant himself. Even I know when to accept defeat.

Of course, whenever black deliverymen delayed us, he pointed out how right he was in his first racial epithet but when white drivers blocked our progress he pretended not to notice. He also had no explanation for why these fabulously wealthy Jewish men were in jeans and work shirts delivering produce. Was this just a millionaire's mitzvah? My driver's large family, of course, bore no resemblance to the overly fertile Latin families. Prejudice rarely involves self-criticism.

Prejudice becomes its own logic and it seeks only confirmation of bias until it is so deeply rooted that it is almost impossible to expel from our unconscious assumptions. With a few hours to kill before the wedding rehearsal, I walked three miles through the fabulous blend of diverse smells, colors, music, and languages that make me love being in New York City. I made my way down to what has been called "ground zero" where the new Freedom Tower now stands. Tourists gather in an old church graveyard next to the construction fences where prayers and meditations have been tied to the branches of trees.

I have always been shocked by the ferocity of prejudices expressed by some in my hometown, since our population is so very white and it is rare even to find opportunities for racial provocation. I have wanted to believe that if only my neighbors had the opportunity to know and experience more racial diversity such prejudices would evaporate. Of course, I also want to believe that most people who do live in the racial diversity of New York City are not as embittered by prejudice as was my frustrated driver. But the one thought that dominated my own prayers as I stood in that graveyard looking up at the newly constructed tower is that prejudice is ultimately a choice and letting go of hatred, resentment, fear, and condescension must also be a choice. One path leads to repeating cycles of violence and war, and the other leads in the direction of mutual understanding and peace. There is no "eye for an eye" solution for the prejudices that plague our world. There is only forgiveness.

Perpetuating the Insane War on Drugs

> Do you believe that there are real medical reasons to use marijuana, or do people use illness as an excuse to have access to an otherwise illegal drug?
>
> Does the prospect of legalizing marijuana sales for recreational purposes seem like a good or bad idea to you?

If marijuana is decriminalized in the United States, should those who are currently incarcerated for possession of marijuana be pardoned and released? Should their criminal record be cleared of these previous charges?

"You want to buy something to make this a really great experience?" The young Mexican from whom I had just purchased a parasailing outing during a Cancun vacation was trying to add to his profits by selling me a little weed to prepare for my brief flight over the ocean. I may be one of the only people who spent the 70's and 80's on college campuses who never smoked pot or used any illegal substance, and I wasn't about to change that policy risking a stay in a Mexican jail. But the fact is that marijuana is pervasive in the world today. It is still illegal in most places, but that has not stopped it from surpassing tobacco as the main cash crop in my native Kentucky, nor has that kept it off of the streets of all American cities.

The "War on Drugs" has been, in this sense, a colossal failure. It has filled our jails, consumed the resources of law enforcement, turned casual drug users into criminals, and yet it has failed to rid our cities of the scourge of the drug trade and the associated cost in lives and treatment dollars for addiction.

I've been counseling people with addiction issues for three decades, since my first grad school clinical in a VA treatment center, and yet I have never encountered anyone in need of counseling who was simply an occasional pot smoker. The solutions to our societal problems with drug abuse will be a complex combination of personal responsibility, appropriate laws, and effective treatment methods.

We are spending a great deal of time and money trying to stamp out a pervasive and less harmful drug while highly addictive and life destroying drugs are still sold legally, albeit in a manner which is clearly skirting the intent of the law. I am referring to the growing practice of selling cocaine and methamphetamine substitutes as plant fertilizers and bath salts. A tiny package of bath salts, clearly marked "Not for Human Consumption" can pack the wallop of street quality cocaine and even though it sells for the same price as street cocaine, this ruse goes on with little or no legal impediment.

Arresting pot smokers while allowing businesses to legally sell a form of meth under the guise of plant food is a nearly insane misdirection of resources. Our police officers know about this drug trade, but they do not have either the laws or the resources to stop it. With considerable regret, speaking as someone who would prefer to remove all such drugs from society, I believe that it is time for our country to redirect our energy in the war on drugs to focus on the drugs that are addicting and killing people and to decriminalize marijuana. I say that not because I think pot is harmless, but because I am convinced that its danger is so far removed from the dangers of cocaine and meth as to be unworthy of our attention.

There are medical and commercial benefits to be found in hemp, and at the recreational level, the difference between the use of alcohol and the use of pot seems only to stress our social hypocrisy. Marijuana is not without its problems, as is true for guns, fast food, cars, alcohol, and prescription medications, but it is time to stop singling out this one herb for special persecution.

The Occupy Wall Street Protests

> As income disparity has become one of the greatest challenges to America's future, the emergence of the Occupy Wall Street movement was easily understandable. However, it is somewhat mystifying that no similar movement emerged after the winter of 2011. What happened to all of that energy?
>
> The Occupy movement was broadly criticized for not having recognizable leadership or appointed spokespersons. Was their attempt at organic democracy a mistake or were they on to something?
>
> In the buildup to the 2016 presidential election, Senator Bernie Sanders is drawing larger crowds than any other candidate because his message echoes the concerns of the Occupy movement, but the media seems to be entirely dismissive of him. What makes Sanders seem like a symbolic candidate while the media seemed to take Donald Trump seriously?

One Sunday afternoon in the summer of 2011, I stood on a busy street corner with parishioners and other demonstrators in solidarity with the Occupy Wall Street movement. There were more than one hundred of us holding signs in peaceful demonstration for the 99 percent of Americans who are in economic insecurity. That week, I joined with church members to feed the unsheltered homeless of our town. A pregnant woman in line told me that she would deliver sometime today. Ignoring the Biblical imagery of a tent-dwelling teenager delivering her first child, I have been gripped by thoughts of what this child's future will be.

Much of the corporate owned media (and the basically corporately-owned politicians) derided the demonstrations on Wall Street, saying that their message lacked focus and that they were unorganized. And to prove their point, they often broadcasted "person on the street" interviews with someone who was clueless as to why they were there. But the ridicule was absurd and painfully hypocritical. Does our Congress appear to be focused and well organized? The international media did a much better job of reporting actual published declarations and interviewing intelligent examples of demonstrators. Our politicians and journalists chose to act confused. The substantive issue is that they intentionally protect the status quo; it is not that they are too dense to understand the protests, it is that they could not afford to admit that they understood.

As Gandhi said, "At first they will ignore us. Then they will make fun of us. Then they will fight us. Then we will win." Domestic media tried to ignore the Occupy Wall Street demonstrators at first. Then they spent a couple of months making fun of them. Then the NYPD engaged in aggressive police tactics, and Mayor Bloomberg took measures to make it illegal to peacefully assemble. Eventually, a harsh winter and aggressive policing ended the movement.

Their message was not vague nor did it lack focus. The primary issue was the shift of wealth in America into the hands of a smaller and smaller minority and the fact that real political power has followed the money. The demands of the demonstrators were complex, because getting the money out of politics and restoring a sane, job-creating economy replete with livable wages, access to housing, healthcare, transportation, and education is very complicated, but more than that, it is necessary.

No one less than the former Federal Reserve chairman, Alan Greenspan, has said that our current income inequality is endangering the survival of capitalism. In fact, the last time there was such a dramatic shift of wealth into the hands of the few, the world was plunged into the Great Depression. The current Fed chairman, Ben Bernanke, has warned that the income disparity is creating two societies. Both political parties have been equally useless in the fight to correct this problem. Now the 99 percent need to find their voice.

9

Gun Control

"Here's an analogy folks, I ask you to think of this: You folks in Chicago, want me to get castrated because your families are having too many kids. It spells out exactly what is happening here! You want us to get rid of guns . . . " To quote Mike Myers' character, Austin Powers, "Paging Dr. Freud!" Here we get to the heart of gun control resistance: anxiety about either losing or having inadequate boy parts.

America after Sandy Hook

We demand progress in automobile safety in the engineering of roads and cars but why can we not apply this engineering skill to gun safety?

If the 30,000 gun deaths in America every year have not prompted sensible gun control legislation, how many casualties would it take to change our thinking? Would 300,000 deaths or 3,000,000 be enough?

Since it is abundantly apparent that the gun industry's political donations keep gun legislation from ever being seriously discussed, could we make it illegal for the gun industry to lobby Congress?

Approximately 3,000 Americans died in a terrorist attack on Sept. 11, 2001. In response to that attack, Congress passed the Patriot Act, sharply curtailing aspects of the Bill of Rights, and President George W. Bush launched two wars, invading and overthrowing the governments of two sovereign states because of their alleged sympathy with the terrorists who attacked us. By the time these wars are paid for, we will have spent trillions of dollars and sacrificed thousands of American lives to answer the threat of terrorism.

Of course, more than 30,000 Americans die from gunshot wounds every year. After the Sandy Hook tragedy in December 2012, it seemed like our country was ready to finally do something about our dangerous gun laws. But as the old saying goes, "When all was said and done, much more was said than done." What has happened to our sensible response to the nightmarish murder of these schoolchildren?

There has certainly been a lot of conversation about gun control legislation, but nothing passed (compare that to the speed with which we responded to 9-11), and the legislation that failed in the Senate was so full of loopholes that it would not deter any but the most ignorant terrorist or criminal who wanted to buy a gun.

Nothing in the proposed Senate bill would have had the slightest impact on stopping the slaughter in Newtown, yet even this watered-down law could not get passed in the National Rifle Association-controlled Congress.

Ironically, we did not find the moral outrage to outlaw assault rifles and large-volume ammunition magazines – far from it! Instead, sales of these weapons have gone through the roof. In fact, in some instances, the price paid for the kind of assault rifles used to murder those schoolchildren more than doubled

This is not inflammatory propaganda. It is a matter of mathematical fact that nothing increases the profits of gun manufacturers more than mass murder because the paranoid reaction of the population is not to outlaw these dangerous weapons, but to buy more, out of erroneous fear that they will become less available.

Resistance to background checks and registries is so intense that even the most facile efforts to keep lethal weapons out of the hands of criminals and the mentally ill is met with the mantra that "Obama is going to take away our guns." One wonders if gun buyers ever get tired of transferring so much of their money into the hands of gun manufacturers, responding to the misinformation of the industry's organ-grinding arm, the NRA, while absolutely nothing has been done by Obama or anyone else to take anyone's guns, not ever, not anywhere!

Even gun control advocates are quick to say that Americans have a gun culture that cannot be significantly changed. The Germans, who gave the world the Holocaust, and the Japanese, who gave us Pearl Harbor, have made a complete transformation from their violent past. In most years, The United States has about 15,000 homicides, Germany has about 150, and Japan has fewer than 10. This amazing metamorphosis has taken place in the course of a single lifetime!

Are they just smarter or more moral than we are capable of becoming? Twenty-five years ago Americans smoked cigarettes in college classrooms, restaurants, airplanes, and even hospital rooms, but we changed all of that so that a guy can't even find a place to enjoy a cigar in the winter without freezing to death. Americans can change, and have changed dramatically in matters we previously would have believed to be impossible. The same can happen with guns. We do not have to accept the massacre of Americans by gun violence. The people of Germany and Japan are not the only civilized, intelligent people in the world.

Mental Health and Gun Ownership

> Most people would be opposed to allowing people with serious mental illnesses to have access to lethal weapons but how can such obvious logic be articulated in gun regulations without further punishing the already stigmatized people who suffer from mental illnesses?
>
> If people who clearly have addiction or mental health problems do manage to get their hands on guns, what is the background check all about?
>
> Why is it asking too much to ask to require a complete psychological work up before issuing a permit for purchasing a lethal weapon? And why wouldn't we require that test to be renewed every four or five years?

Every time there is another senseless massacre committed by a madman armed with military-styled weapons, there is an article in me that fights to come out. I want to scream at the people who donate to the National Rifle Association, which uses lobbyists and campaign dollars to keep politicians on a diamond-encrusted leash, doing its bidding, preventing all sane restrictions against the availability of assault rifles and high-round ammo clips.

Though everyone agrees that the mentally unstable should not be allowed to buy lethal weapons, what more diagnostic criteria is needed other than the desire to own an assault rifle with a fifty-round ammo drum? What else does a person have to do—serve red wine with fish?

But I have written that article, more than once. I know the familiar steps of the dance . . . We have a right to bear arms . . . Guns don't kill people, people kill people. For the people who make these arguments, the knowledge that a three-month-old baby was shot does not make them question the availability of assault rifles; it makes them ask why a mother had taken a three-month-old out to a movie at midnight—as if the mother deserved to have her child shot because of her irresponsibility.

I sleep with the news on. It is a bad habit, I know, but a habit I am not inclined to kick. But when I am awakened by another report of a mass murder, I do not sleep well again for many days. On Thursdays, I maintain the discipline of joining with other volunteers to serve lunch to the ever-growing numbers of my hometown's homeless. In the summer months, the shelter gets hot as the air conditioning cannot keep up while a hundred people crowd into the small space we have, and we bring in warm food. The only comfort is the practice of compassion. I cannot make those who would make military firepower available to the public see the insanity of that policy, but I can return to the task of putting another ladle full of compassion into the darkness.

There is an old Buddhist saying: Before enlightenment, I chop wood; I carry water. After enlightenment, I chop wood; I carry water. In a world gone mad, giving ourselves to the basic acts of kindness we are capable of may be the only way to hold on to sanity.

There will always be members of society who are mentally ill. That is an unchangeable fact. Often, their first undeniably display of insanity is when they have murdered several men, women, children and infants. I grieve the fact that assault rifles are more available than appropriate mental healthcare. I grieve the rush to defend the weapons that could be controlled, and the inclination to blame that uncontrollable but foreseeable occurrence of a mind that goes perilously off-track. Other nations have solved this problem; in fact, almost all industrialized nations have done so.

Until we rise to that level of moral responsibility, I try to put some light back into a dark world in the only ways that I can, through acts of compassion. I chop wood. I carry water.

Is the National Rifle Association a Domestic Terrorist Organization?

> In the past few years, contrary to the impression left by excessive media attention, only one American died from Ebola, three at the hands of Isis on the battlefield, and even Al Qaeda, who drove the United States into the longest war in American history, can claim no more than 3500 victims. How can the NRA continue to lobby for virtually non-existent gun laws and not be identified as an enemy of America when more than a million Americans have died from gunshot wounds over the last generation?
>
> More than half of our domestic gun deaths are suicides. Does that somehow make the number less staggering to you?
>
> Domestic fights and suicide attempts are much more likely to be lethal if there is a gun present. Can you imagine how America might be different if guns were not kept in residences?

All too often I begin my day by reading a newspaper story about another local shooting, or a murder-suicide, and sometimes even an entire family killed in the midst of a domestic fight. Reading these accounts, I relive the horror and sorrow I have felt every time I have had to prepare a funeral for a member of my church who died violently at the hands of a spouse or by suicide.

In thirty-five years of parish ministry, I have lost five parishioners to gun violence. During my time as a hospital chaplain, when I was in graduate school, I was assigned to the neurosurgery ward of a VA hospital where we typically had four or five patients who had shot themselves in the head, but who had not immediately died.

Four of the five parishioners I have lost, and most of the hospital patients I cared for, were shot on impulse. Only one of the deaths was a planned murder. One of my best friends, who had struggled with clinical depression for years, placed a call to a repairman to come fix her dishwasher. Then she called her lawn service to come rake leaves, and only then went to the hall closet, retrieved her husband's loaded revolver, stepped out into the back yard, and shot herself in the head. Like most suicides, it happened in a moment, and could easily have been prevented if a gun were not so readily available.

In Great Britain, you can own a gun, but you have to keep it secured at a gun club. Gun-related murder and suicide still happen in Great Britain, but not on impulse. You have to go get your weapon while the gun club is open for business, and apparently, that has worked to make gun related suicide and murder in Great Britain about one thousand times rarer than it is in the United States. Faced with overwhelming evidence for how well gun control works in Japan, Great Britain, Australia, and other advanced countries, the fact that American politicians have not been able to do anything to protect our citizens from such tragedies is inexplicable. I hope it is not the NRA political donations but I'm afraid that it is the NRA political donations. Okay . . . It is the political influence of the NRA that is directly responsible for 30,000 American deaths a year, and so what moral politician would ever accept another contribution from such a blood-drenched organization?

Since our government lacks the moral integrity to take meaningful action, families really must choose to act in their own best interests. Gun owners, sometimes with the help and support of family and friends, must choose to securely store their weapons somewhere other than their home, if they are at risk of murder or suicide. Who should not keep a weapon in his or her home? Based on my experience with losses, I believe that homes where there has been a history of mental illness, where anyone is taking antidepressants, where there has been domestic abuse, or alcohol or drug abuse, or where anyone is undergoing unusual stress from unemployment, marital infidelity, divorce, or rape should not have lethal weapons close at hand. I urge gun owners to love their families and care for themselves enough not to keep their guns at home when there is substantive risk of murder or suicide.

Big Guns for Little Dicks

> There is a common assumption that guns are phallic symbols that ease the insecurity of men about their masculinity. If this is true, what might be a less lethal way of dealing with that insecurity?

> Many people claim that they keep a gun in their home to protect their family, when statistics make it clear that having a gun in the house makes it many times more likely that someone in that house will die from a gunshot. The claim of self-protection is not logical, but how can one get around the emotional need for what gun owners believe increases their security?

Many non-lethal weapons are available to the police that are not available to the average citizen. Why can you buy a gun that shoots bullets, but you cannot buy a gun that shoots beanbags?

The most common dreams are anxiety dreams. The falling and chasing dreams of early childhood give way to what is called the "test anxiety dream," or that other intensely uncomfortable dream in which you find yourself in a public place either naked or in your underwear. These later two dreams reflect an unconscious fear that you may be inadequate, and that your inadequacy is about to be discovered. Most teens and young adults have one or both of these dreams, but thankfully, they usually subside once we have found our role in life and come to have more self-confidence.

Grown men repress it so much that they don't generally remember it, but little boys who are just at the point of discovering themselves often realize an irrational fear that their mother or sister will, out of jealousy, remove their uniquely male appendage. Granting an exception for anyone in a relationship with Lorena Bobbitt, this castration anxiety, like the Oedipal and Elektra complexes of early childhood, tends to resolve itself . . . in most cases.

I and many other commentators on America's epidemic of gun violence have frequently commented on the unconscious connection between a man's guns and a man's boy parts. With all due respect to the many editors with whom I have worked at the *Springfield NewsLeader* over the past decades, my insistence upon the association between fear of castration and anger about gun control has not often made its way into ink no matter how much hard (no double entendre intended) evidence there is to support the claim.

Thankfully, we now have a self-evident connection made by an Illinois legislator, Jim Sacia (R), who, during a gun control debate, said, "Here's an analogy folks, I ask you to think of this: You folks in Chicago, want me to get castrated because your families are having too many kids. It spells out exactly what is happening here! You want us to get rid of guns . . . "[1] To quote Mike Myers' character, Austin Powers, "Paging Dr. Freud!" Here we get to the heart of gun control resistance: anxiety about losing or having inadequate boy parts.

The seemingly impossible impasse in Congress is because we continually try to approach gun control from a direct logical argument about the huge death toll and the entirely unnecessary proliferation of assault weapons, large count ammo magazines, and handguns. This sort of logic

1. Before It's News, "IL State Representative Compares Chicago Gun Laws to Castration."

never addresses the two real motivations for most of gun ownership, both of which are irrational and logic-proof: the exaggerated fear of one's neighbors and an unresolved childhood fear of castration, or perhaps an adult fear of being discovered to be inadequate.

Here are two facts that must preface the next step in the gun control debate:

1. Having a gun in your home, except in the most rare cases, makes you less safe rather than more safe. I know that you think you know how to store and handle a weapon, and so do the owners of the guns used in more than 100,000 shootings in America every year. The proliferation of guns in homes is inescapably linked to the high incidences of gun casualties. It's just a fact.

2. Research has proven that no matter how many guns you collect, your private parts will not grow larger or stronger. So, those anxieties aside, what can we do together to reduce the death toll from gun violence in America?

James Brady and Gabby Giffords Speak to America

After two terms in office, where are all of the guns that Obama took from Americans?

NRA spokesman Wayne LaPierre tried frightening voters into believing that Obama would "take your guns," and even though Obama never did, during the next presidential campaign, he warned voters that Hillary would take their guns. Does there ever come a time that such claims become obviously false to gun owners?

The NRA advocates for guns to be in elementary schools, high schools, and college campuses to prevent mass shootings, but they do not allow their members to carry firearms into NRA conventions. Why is that?

On a chilly fall day in 2008, I sat alone at a table in one of our fair city's west side dives that still allowed a gentleman to enjoy a hand rolled Nicaraguan cigar. I was listening to the TV news but could not help overhearing the man at the next table trying to persuade the young woman sitting with him not to vote for Barack Obama. Though he agreed with his female companion's insistence that the country had been poorly administered under George W. Bush and that we needed a change, he cautioned her in the most somber tone imaginable, "The day that Obama takes office he will take away all of our guns."

Of course, nothing could have been further from the truth, yet such scare tactics have been used in every election to try to keep only NRA-approved candidates in office. Only President Bill Clinton has made even the slightest dent in the availability of assault weapons in the past generation and the important assault weapon ban which he signed in 1994, expired in 2004. President Bush was even unwilling to curtail the availability of ammunition clips that hold more than ten rounds, making the shooting sprees such as the ones we have witnessed in recent years much more deadly.

Clinton also signed the Brady Bill, which requires a five-day waiting period to purchase a handgun—unless of course, you are buying at a gun show, a flea market, or from an individual. All of which goes to say that America has virtually no gun laws. While I grew up owning guns and was a part of the hunting culture of my native Kentucky, after losing a couple of church members to gun violence, my sympathies were curbed. After spending five hours with a double-barreled shotgun pointed at my face, held by one of my less successful addiction counseling clients, my desire for meaningful gun control laws was solidified.

A couple of years after my own close brush with sudden death, when I had begun to sleep through the night again, the survival of James Brady, who had been struck by a bullet during a failed assassination attempt on Ronald Reagan, prompted a public debate on who should be allowed to own a gun and what kinds of guns should be available to the public. Had Brady died in the shooting as tens of thousands of Americans do every year, his death would likely have been quickly forgotten. It was his courageous lobbying, with the assistance of his wife that finally saw some progress towards sanity in American gun laws.

We can hope that Congresswoman Gabby Giffords' survival may give new life to a reasonable debate that has been kept off the floor of the Congress by NRA donations. Somewhere between the rights of hunters and those who need a weapon for self-protection and the access to assault weapons by the insane, a responsible government is supposed to draw a line. That line has not yet been drawn. May God bless Gabby.

Assault Rifle Sales in the Aftermath of Mass Murder

> People who have mental illness suffer from many unfair and challenging social stigmas. How can we work to avoid allowing people who have a mental illness that might lead to gun violence from having access to guns while not adding to the burden of their unjust social stigmas?

> Aware gun shop employees who refused to sell ammunition to a customer who seemed to be behaving suspiciously have thwarted some murders. However, some mass murderers have simply gone online to buy large volumes of ammunition. Shouldn't online purchases of guns and ammunition be illegal?

> Since there are no background checks or standards for those who buy weapons at gun shows, should we even allow assault rifles to be in circulation? Why is there a gun show loophole at all?

In the weeks following the Sandy Hook massacre, our divided nation reacted in two distinctly different ways. There was an outpouring of generosity shown to the survivors in Connecticut and a resurgence of interest in enacting gun control, while at the same time retail stores immediately sold out of their supply of weapons and ammunition. Seeing how a solitary shooter can take an assault rifle with a large ammo magazine into a school and create a bloody nightmare, one person thinks, "What can I do to comfort the bereaved and keep this from happening again?" and another chillingly says, "I want one of those guns."

The gap between the gun enthusiasts and those who want to more tightly regulate firearms is nowhere better displayed than on the opinion pages of Midwestern newspapers. In a letter to the editor that appeared in my hometown paper, a retired policeman cited the fact that there had been an attack in a school in China on the same day as the attack at Sandy Hook. His point was that strict gun laws in China had not prevented an insane man from attacking defenseless children and therefore gun laws are inconsequential in these tragedies.

It read like a script from *Saturday Night Live*. The author had no apparent appreciation for the fact that because there were no guns involved in the school tragedy in China, there were no deaths in that incident, while there were twenty children murdered in Connecticut. How do you reason with people who are so emphatic in their support of gun ownership that the difference between no children being killed and twenty children being killed is not significant?

A comedian asks, "How many NRA members does it take to change a light bulb?" And the answer from the NRA crowd is, "More guns." If, in the face of tens of thousands of senseless deaths, any group of people insists that the answer is always "more guns," then they have removed themselves from rational conversation.

Another letter to the editor appearing on the same day as the one mentioned above made the tired suggestion that the solution to school security is to arm everyone over the age of sixteen, as if the author was unaware of the presence of drug and alcohol abuse in school populations, or even the sheer impulsivity of teens. It is akin to saying that the solution to the problem of drunk driving is for drivers to drink more. Sure, guns don't kill without a person using the gun, but a person with a gun is much more likely to kill than a person without a gun. In America, we have over 30,000 gun deaths per year, while many other nations have so few that you can count them on your fingers. There is no logical denial of the fact that the proliferation of guns in our country is the single most manageable factor in this horrifying annual bloodbath.

2012 became the first year in half a century when gun deaths outnumbered auto deaths in our nation, and still the enthusiasts are demanding that there be no changes made in our gun laws even if we have to spend billions of dollars to add armed guards to public schools—nothing can come between gun enthusiasts and their weapons. It is time for the grown-ups among us to take responsibility for duplicating the best practices seen in other developed nations in the recalcitrant, bloody, gun-loving United States.

Religious, Philosophical, and Personal

10

Faith and Practice

We are morally compelled to agree on compassion so that we can find a highest common denominator of service rather than the lowest common denominator of doctrine.

The Evolution of Faith

Do religious holidays ever motivate you to make substantive changes in your life?

Beyond all matters of vanity (losing weight, accomplishing a personal goal) what would you "give up" for Lent to make yourself a better person?

Progressives are notorious individualists. Have we lost something in not being in any way accountable to a faith community for our personal morality?

Progressive Christian churches often shy away from traditional services and overt religious symbols, especially the cross, because of the negative associations with orthodox theology regarding substitutionary death, Trinitarian beliefs, or the divinity of Jesus. Some have written voluminously about getting rid of the cross because it has negative implications of suffering and death (as if we could stop death from happening if only we would stop making coffins).

For me, the cross is a historical fact before it is a religious symbol. Jesus of Nazareth was murdered by the Roman occupation forces because of his subversive preaching. Since then, countless others have had to make huge sacrifices to keep his message of radical compassion from being swallowed up in the self-absorbed values of culture. The cross isn't magic; it is a reality.

The church where I am a pastor is an interfaith community. We are of a largely Christian heritage, but we have active members who continue to consider themselves to be Jewish, Buddhist, or even agnostic. The cross that hangs in our sanctuary does not mean that we are exclusively Christian, but that we embrace the message and the real history of Jesus.

Which brings me, by way of circumlocution, to the topic of Ash Wednesday. An Ash Wednesday service involves prayers of repentance, assurance of pardon and a fairly bizarre ritual of having a cross of palm ashes rubbed on your forehead in spite of the very clear gospel injunction to not disfigure your face when you are in a time of penitence.

When I was in a traditional denomination and I reached out with dusty ashes on my thumb to mark the next person in line, I repeated a sentence that priests and pastors have said to their parishioners for centuries: "Remember that you are dust and to the dust you shall return." Try looking into the eyes of a guy who everyone knows is weeks away from death and saying that to him! I've done it and it is a shocking exercise.

And yet, it is a fact. Eventually, we are all going to turn to dust. On Ash Wednesday, we come to grips with our mortality and all of the imperfections that come with it. I don't observe Lent, but I know that it can be a time to make a new resolution to change the direction of your mortal life.

There is a Japanese proverb that says, "The day you decide to do it is your lucky day." Ash Wednesday could be the lucky day that an alcoholic decides to stop drinking. It could be the day when a couple that once pledged to love and honor one another until parted by death comes to realize that it is time to stop fighting.

As a progressive liberal, I no longer observe Ash Wednesday but I recognize that life is, at best, very short, and I am not yet the man I long to be and I hope that I can muster the strength to make another step towards becoming that person. I don't need a holy day or a ritual to make today my lucky day but I, and you, do need to find a day on which we make that crucial decision to change. The mortality rate is still 100 percent and so, realizing that my total number of days is limited, I need to decorate my life with lucky days.

Seeking the Highest Common Denominator

> Religious people seem to have a hard time getting along with one another. How far should we go to tolerate our differences in order to work together on common causes?
>
> Habitat for Humanity's founder, Millard Fuller, was fond of talking about the "theology of the hammer," saying that conservatives and liberals, Catholics and Protestants, Christians and Jews, should be able to find the common ground of helping the poor that is common to all of our faith traditions. Would you join a building team on a Habitat site whose religious views were in opposition to your own?
>
> Have you found yourself staying in a religious community because of your social connections there, even though you do not feel that you have much in common with their stated beliefs?

Growing up as a liberal in the south, I've been accustomed to being in a very small minority. However, as a member of the clergy, I felt that it was my duty to participate in the gatherings of the community's Ministerial Alliance even though I often came away from those meetings feeling that I was very out of place. The first Ministerial Alliance meeting I attended when I had moved to my adopted state of Missouri was in the fall of 1991. There were about two hundred ministers at that meeting. A particularly conservative pastor sat across the table from me, and after a short introduction, he began to explain to me why I, and members of my denomination, were in open rebellion against God because of our tolerance of homosexuality. He didn't convince me to share his prejudice against gays, but he did convince me to stop going to preachers' meetings.

A decade later, when I decided to give it another try, I discovered that there had been a sea change in the constituency of these meetings. When I returned to the Ministerial Alliance there were two other pastors of congregations and about a half-dozen retired pastors. At that time I was promoting a project to build houses for the poor of Nicaragua. I had hoped to promote that project in gatherings of ministers, but the fact was, by the early twenty-first century, pastors rarely gathered outside of their own denominational groups.

No one much grieved the passing of obligatory preacher meetings, yet there are things that we can do together that we cannot do alone, and we cannot do those things if we cannot stand to be in regular conversation. Clearly, expecting the clergy to provide a role model of tolerance in order to accomplish important goals seems like a given. Still, we don't do it well, and we don't do it very often.

With growing poverty in this sour economy, it is increasingly incumbent upon churches to work together even if they do not agree on biblical interpretation, sacraments, or salvation. We are morally compelled to agree on compassion so that we can find a highest common denominator of service rather than the lowest common denominator of doctrine.

Ethical Opinions with No "Skin in the Game"

> Historians differ as the reason why Jesus of Nazareth was executed by the Roman government, but one thing is certain—he was not crucified for being a moderate. What religious views do you hold that might be so radical that it would make established religions, the banking system, or the government to wish that you were dead?
>
> Have you ever risked your employment by taking a moral stand on any issue? Do you articulate your passionately held views in such a way as to alienate any friendships or family relationships?
>
> What is the largest personal sacrifice that you have ever made to help a stranger?

Dietrich Bonhoeffer, that famous martyr of the anti-Hitler movement, spoke often of the church's love for "cheap grace." True discipleship, he said, had a cost and, in Bonhoeffer's case, the cost was his life. He was not content to console himself with the earnest conviction that Hitler's program of ethnic cleansing was wrong, but rather he left the safety of the United States, returned to Germany, and became involved in a plot to assassinate Hitler—a plot that was discovered, resulting in Bonhoeffer's execution.

It seems to me that much of the chest-thumping that passes for religion on the editorial pages of the local newspapers is little more than cheap religious gossip. For the past couple of generations, we've been blessed by an abundance of religious people who tell us that they have been "born again," a reference to the conversation Jesus had with Nicodemus in the third chapter of John. This example of Jesus telling a man that he must be "born from above" (literal translation) only appears once in the gospels. However, another encounter is reported three times, once each in Matthew, Mark, and Luke in which Jesus tells a man that he must sell everything he owns and give the money to the poor in order to become a part of God's kingdom.

Now, why are there so many "born again" Christians and so few "gave all I owned to the poor" Christians? Because the later actually requires sacrificial action and the former can be little more than religious narcissism.

Similarly, when a man or a post-menopausal woman writes a letter to the editor condemning abortion, he or she is offering a strong opinion about a topic in which he or she has no "skin in the game." It costs me nothing to have a bold opinion about how you should live your life when it has no implications for my own life. The happily wed can summarily condemn the divorced and the comfortably heterosexual can castigate the homosexual and then pat themselves on the backs for being good Christians, though the exercise appears to be rather cheap and meaningless.

As in Bonhoeffer's case, it is one thing to be ideologically against the Nazis; it is quite another to put your own body in the doorway and tell them to stop the genocide. Are you are opposed to abortion? Good news! You don't have to get one! Are you against homosexuality? Good for you, now all you have to do is refrain from same-sex relationships and you are home free!

The historical Jesus was a liberator of the oppressed, an advocate for the poor, a healer of the sick, and someone who liberally forgave those burdened by the weight of religious guilt. He lived without owning property, and with little more than a glancing involvement in the economy. And so, while I know that I will receive numerous rebukes from the "born again" community, I can tell you that I will give the "I gave all I owned to the poor" folks a lot more credibility.

Can a Spiritual Person Remain Uninformed?

While slavery is part of long-removed history in America, the marketing of slavery-produced goods is alive and well. What is the difference between owning a slave and financially supporting slavery?

Both governments and institutions of religion assume the right to determine right and wrong for us, but what is our own obligation to make those decisions for ourselves?

Can either "my religion teaches" or "I was following orders" serve as an apologetic for prejudice, torture, or indifference in the twenty-first century?

While traveling with church members to see the ancient pyramid at Memphis (how often do you get to work that into a conversation?) the bus pulled over at a warehouse. We were led into a factory where children, five to seven years of age, were sitting at huge looms weaving rugs. There were about a hundred malnourished children working. They were hungry for our attention, begging for food and money.

"Child labor!" I managed to gasp. The tour guide was ready with his defense: "These children are helping to support their families while they learn a trade. This is their school. Without this work they would be starving and illiterate." These were, I pointed out, the exact same arguments proffered by the American textile mills two hundred years ago!

The busload of tourists, all Americans traveling with church groups, pushed past me into the showroom, where even the people who had sat and listened to my social justice sermons for ten years bought Egyptian rugs that had recently been made by poor children whose forced labor they had seen with their own eyes!

I stared at one Bible-thumping Sunday School teacher in disbelief as he snarled, "You heard what he said—those children need for us to buy their wares."

I think of that exchange very often when we wonder how our soldiers could have actually tortured prisoners in Abu Ghraib and Guantanamo. Well, it's like this: they were told to do it by people they assumed knew right from wrong. The larger question is, "How do we get people to think seriously about ethics in the real world?" Anyone should know that torture is wrong or that enslaving children is evil without having to be told, and yet when told that it is not wrong, still, mature adults should have enough trained ethical awareness to stand up to authority and say, "No, that's not right." We should not be fooled into thinking that it is wrong to give healthcare to the sick just because someone says, "Oh, that's socialist!" Nor should we reject efforts at improving education for poor children because "liberals" champion such causes.

During her visit to my hometown, Sister Helen Prejean (author of *Dead Man Walking*) talked about how most us live in a "bubble," unaware of the world around us. We don't know that most of the criminals who are executed are black, or that execution is almost always only sought when the victim was white. We assume that the death penalty deters crime, when it clearly does not. Sister Helen implored the young students at the university where she spoke, and later the same day she begged church members to make themselves aware of the world, and to be courageous enough to act to end injustice and poverty.

Prejean described the path we all need to follow (especially among the religious) from passive acceptance of the status quo toward becoming ethically aware actors on the world stage.

It's Not History!

> Can the fostering of community and encouragement to ethical living found in formal religion survive the death of ancient myths and creeds?

> A more rational and academic approach to religion has taken hold in both Europe and in the Americas in previous generations, but the Enlightenment on both continents seemed to fade and give way to resurgence of faith in Iron Age myths. Will the twenty-first century witness the final death of traditional Judaism, Christianity, and Islam?

> More meditative and less theistic forms of faith seem to be taking root in the United States, often in Humanist discussion groups, Yoga studios, and Buddhist meditation meetings. Will these less formal and doctrinal practices eclipse traditional organized religion?

An animal activist, who had apparently not really understood my lecture on the use of myth in scripture, asked me about the Noah story, "I understand that God killed all of the people on earth because they were evil, but how could God have killed all of those innocent animals?" My animal-loving student was prepared to believe that Noah, at the age of 500, had three sons (Genesis 5:32), and that when he was 600 and his sons were 100 years old (Genesis 7:6), they built a boat large enough to hold two of every kind of animal on earth (plus a few "clean" animals for sacrifice . . . As if dying in a flood was not bad enough). Then, after a dysfunctional family incident, Noah died at the age of 950 (Genesis 9:28-29), leaving behind a global gene pool so shallow that no species could possibly survive. All of this seemed acceptable to her, but killing innocent animals was just stretching credibility too far.

Some Christians, Muslims, and Jews protested the release of a new movie about Noah, and some Muslim countries banned it. What are they upset about? The movie is, according to them, not sufficiently true to the

Biblical account. Yet, as comedian Bill Maher observed, in the Biblical account, God plays the part of genocidal psychopath who kills not just millions of men and women but even infants, because they are . . . wait for it . . . evil babies. I would protest a movie that did stay true to the Biblical story, depicting God as more evil than Genghis Khan, Nero, and Hitler all rolled into one, but traditionalist purists are literally demanding that these ancient myths be treated as history, even if they portray the Lord God Almighty as being the most vicious murderer of all time.

I would have thought that at this time, when traditional religion is in sharp decline, Hollywood would avoid stepping into this arena. But 2014 movie offerings looked like a virtual tent revival in the theaters with the release of *Son of God,* which portrays Jesus in the "You people are so evil God had to kill His own son," role, *Heaven is for Real,* attempting to give evidence for the existence of an eternal afterlife based on the account of a four year old under anesthesia, and *Exodus,* starring Christian Bale as Moses, and again, reportedly treating the Biblical narrative as literal history.

All of which will be used as fodder for comedians to talk about how very gullible, unscientific, and frankly, slow religious people are. People who take a real world approach to global climate change, gender roles, sexual orientation, environmental concerns, and the hazards of modern warfare can look back at their mosques, synagogues, and churches and shake their heads at the anachronistic teachings of religion. Still, as silly as they may appear, those churches, synagogues and mosques started many of our nation's hospitals and homeless shelters, and still do more than any other institution in providing direct aid to the poor and to war refugees and disaster victims. Sadly, however, we are not thought of in terms of our radical compassion, but in terms of our commitment to superstition and myth. It is my earnest hope that our personal belief system will become deeper than Hollywood appears to think it is. If it does not, then I fear that faith communities do not have much of a future, and when they go, they will likely take most of their good deeds with them, and we will live in a harder and less civilized world.

Can Feeding the Hungry Be a Religious Sacrament?

In the practice of your religion, which is more important, what you believe or what you do?

Even during prohibition, exceptions were made for certain religious services to legally serve wine. Can progressive religious people claim a freedom of religion exception to municipal laws against feeding the poor in public places?

Which is the more important part of the life of Jesus, the body of his teachings or the death of his body?

There is often a conflict between retail businesses and the places where the presence of homeless services causes the poor to congregate in urban areas. I am sympathetic with business owners who do not want customers scared away because the homeless are gathered around their store. However, the increasingly common practice of arresting people for feeding homeless populations seems like a direct infringement of the free practice of religion. Though care for the poor is a part of most expressions of Christianity, for those of us who practice a progressive faith, involvement in social justice causes is central to our religion.

Unlike traditional Christians, I do not believe that the Bible is the word of God. I do not believe that Jesus was divine in ways that you and I are not. I do not believe in a supernatural, theistic God who enters human history, healing some and allowing others to die, blessing the Cardinals while loathing the Cubs. I don't believe in a final judgment, souls, or a literal heaven and hell.

My interest in Jesus is not in what was said about him, but rather it is in what he is believed to have said as a teacher of morality and a reformer of society. Just like such authors as Bishop John Shelby Spong, Marcus Borg, and Karen Armstrong, I believe that Jesus was the teacher of radical compassion and it is in the practice of radical compassion that a person actually becomes a Christian. I realize that what I have said will not even sound like Christianity to traditionalists, but fortunately, just as they get to define their faith for themselves, I get to define mine for myself.

For me, and for many progressives, the practice of faith is much more important than personal beliefs. There is an old African proverb that says, "When you pray, move your feet." Progressives do not put much stock in simply reciting intercessory prayers in church services or silently inside our heads. For us, prayer is more a matter of doing.

Yes, we have beliefs, and we strive to articulate those beliefs as courageously, even as prophetically, as possible. We believe in justice, mercy, forgiveness, love, and grace. We believe that sin has much more to do with the violence of war, poverty, racism, discrimination, and the destruction of the planet than it has to do with the victimless sins of consensual sexual relationships, cursing, drinking, and dancing. (I personally think that the way I dance is sinful, but only because I have no sense of rhythm.)

Just as you learn to ride a bicycle by riding a bicycle and you learn to sing by singing, we believe that our faith only becomes real when we practice it by direct and personal involvement. Read the book of James in the New Testament for more information. So we cook food in our homes to share a hot meal with a couple of hundred homeless people every week, in order to treat them in much the same way that we treat our families and ourselves. If you were to attend one of the Sunday services where I am the pastor, you might be surprised to see that we continue to include communion in our gatherings, but not as a sacrament. For us, it is a reminder of the prophetic vision of the great Kingdom feast where everyone has a place at the table in the reign of God, when there will not be some who are hungry and others who are overfed, where there will not be some who are homeless and others who own mansions or multiple dwellings. For us, communion is a sign of unity with the poor.

I have lived downtown in my hometown. I sympathize with business owners and loft dwellers who do not want to feel threatened or harassed by panhandlers, vagrants and addicts. I'm just saying that for me, a war on poverty makes more moral sense than a war on the poor.

Liberation from Literalism

From the time of Augustine, there have been religious scholars who taught that such things as the Genesis account of a talking snake and the story of Jonah living in the belly of a fish for three days were metaphorical. Why then does every century seem to see a majority of religious people falling back into literalism?

Thomas Paine, an early American thinker, insisted that nature was the only reliable "word of God," and that moderns must reject the authority of scriptures that were, not written by their purported authors, describing events that never happened. In the presence of such cynical thought about scripture in the early days of the American nation, why did the public ignore such scholarship to return to a more ancient acceptance of the authority of scriptures?

A debate among religious people goes to the relative importance of orthodoxy (right beliefs) or orthopraxy (right actions). Which do you believe is more important?

Most semesters, I teach a course for one or more of our area colleges on the major religions of the western world. We trace the cross-pollinating influences of Zoroastrianism on post-exilic Judaism, how both gave birth to Christianity, and all three influenced the evolution of Islam. All four of these major religions originated among an impoverished and oppressed people, and initially stressed the sacred value of all human life and the equality of all people.

Each religion eventually sought to give some response to the painful and frightening existential awareness that everyone eventually dies. Later generations attempt to bolster the importance of their founders and prophets by recording accounts of their alleged miracles. Typically, it is not difficult for students reared in the Midwest to read the account of Mohammed's night ride on a winged horse from Mecca to the temple in Jerusalem, and finally to heaven, as a metaphor or a vision. There is, after all, no such thing as flying horses and there was no temple in Jerusalem during the time of Mohammed. We can be very analytical about these facts.

But when you consider something such as the account in the Christian New Testament about Jesus telling Peter to go catch a fish and that he will find a coin in the fish's mouth to be used to pay the Temple tax for Jesus and Peter (Matthew 17:27), it is harder to be so objective. It is difficult for someone who grew up in the environment of evangelical Christianity to read the Christian Bible with the same rational analysis with which he or she reads Zoroastrian or Muslim texts, just as it would be difficult for that magical fish to be objective about water.

The Apostle Paul, the first person to write portions of the New Testament, makes no claim about there being an empty tomb in Jerusalem from which Jesus was raised. He makes no claim of having literally seen Jesus, but only that he had a vision, and in fact, he seems to imply that a vision is all anyone else ever saw of Jesus (I Corinthians 15:5-8), yet later generations record accounts that are much more corporeal. Paul bemoans the fact that he is not capable of healing even himself, but that he must be content with weakness. Two generations after his death, however, the author of Acts attributes several miracles, including raising the dead, to the historically arrogant apostle who never mentioned accomplishing such feats.

As the world's populations move about both physically and through social media, we will no longer be able to be smug about religious claims that "My religious stories are all literally true and yours are just myths," if we ever hope to get along with one another. Literalism among any of the world's religions leads to sectarian divisions that foster radicals, terrorists, and wars. Yet each of the world's religions brings helpful insights into building character, respect for the lives of others, protection of the poor and the vulnerable, and deep compassion for those who suffer. These are the gifts of our faith traditions to the twenty-first century, if only we can focus on the ethical teachings of faith, and not on the magic and superstition.

The Cross We All Eventually Bear

> If the passion narrative of the New Testament gospels is an archetypal story, with which character in the narrative do you most closely identify?
>
> Some people read the story of the resurrection of Jesus from the dead as a singular historical event. Others see it as a metaphor for surviving a crisis and regaining life. Which way of thinking of the event has the greater impact on a modern life?
>
> Does belief in life after death make it easier to accept and tolerate injustice in this life? If so, are we risking the value of this life, which is certain, for hope in a future existence that may not exist?

The large auditorium classes of undergraduate school give way to much smaller gatherings in grad school, and in the later years, most classes are taught around a conference table with no more than five or six students sitting with the professor. This arrangement leaves nowhere to hide when the professor becomes agitated about something. It was Easter week when my already famous homiletics professor, David Buttrick, yelled at the tiny gathering before him, "Jesus rises from the tomb and we all get to live forever, YIPPEE!"

Buttrick rarely simply disapproved of something. He could describe burned toast as being "vile," and a simple inconvenience as "insipid." So when he wrote "heretical" in the margins of a sermon manuscript, you had to take it in context of a man who was, at least in his own mind, larger than life. But his rage about Easter was much more than his usual passionate overstatement. He felt that the church's Easter traditions had trivialized the larger meaning of the metaphor of resurrection.

Easter, he insisted, contained the message of God overruling the unjust judgments of the world. Jesus, like so many of us, had been betrayed by a close friend. He had suffered the abuse at the hands of his religious community. He had been executed under false allegations in an unjust government trial. No matter whether the gospel account of the passion is literally historical, it is true nonetheless. Not true simply for Jesus, but true for many, if not most of us.

What keeps the story of Jesus' passion so relevant is not because it has happened to Jesus but because it expresses what so many others have gone through. When we read the words, "Judas, must you betray me with a kiss?", we almost never think of some dark bearded first century Palestinian but rather we see in our mind's eye the face of someone who loved us and whom we loved, who has done us great harm.

Thankfully, crucifixion is not legal these days, but we use the language, saying that a former employer "crucified me," or of a group of former friends at the club, "they tried to bury me." The power of the Easter story, for Buttrick (and for many of us) is not an unverifiable claim of eternal life in an unknown and unknowable future. The metaphor of resurrection is here and now. That even if it feels like divorce or unemployment or the death of a parent or estrangement from a grown child is the end of our lives, it is not, or at least, it does not have to be.

The image of a man who was dead and sealed into a tomb, rising up and seeing the stone miraculously rolled away is literal for most of Christendom, but for many of us it is the reassurance that no one—not an employer, not a spouse, parent, child, neighbor, or friend can take our lives away from us if we have the strength to rise up and go on living.

Prophets and Saints among the Occupy Movement

Most Western religions began as a protest movement among the poor against the abuses of the wealthy before those religions were adopted by the ruling class. Can these ancient faiths be restored to their role of prophetic challenge to those who are in power?

Pope Francis seems to be trying to lead the Roman Catholic Church back in the direction of the liberation theology movement it once rejected. Can this pope effectively change the Catholic Church?

151

The founders of Judaism, Christianity, and Islam were from the
poor and oppressed of their day. Would any one of their founders
participate in modern-day Judaism, Christianity, or Islam as they
are now?

Theodore Ludwig, the author of one of the textbooks I use in my Western Religions course, says that "Muslim armies overthrew the Byzantine
overlords, and the peasant population happily accepted the new religion
of equality and justice." That observation about the end of the first mil-
lennium of the Common Era stood out with real clarity in the fall of 2011
when the Occupy Wall Street demonstrations were in the news.

While it is historically true that Muhammad was known for maintaining a very humble lifestyle, wearing worn-out garments and living in
a small house, it was not equally true of the caliphs who succeeded him.
Peasants once experienced Islam as a religion of equality and justice, but
I am not certain that many Middle Eastern peasants would say that today.

Similarly, Jewish tradition has it that their faith came into existence
in the midst of a slave revolt in Egypt. The oppressed ethnic minority of
Egypt fled the cruel exploitation of the pharaohs, and for centuries refused
to have a king because they knew how royalty inevitably exploits the poor.
Once they succumbed to the temptation to install a government like the
governments of their neighbors, the Jewish prophetic tradition becomes
full of angry protests against the king's abuse of the people.

Before it became the royal religion, Zoroastrianism appealed to the
ancient Persians, because it taught that both the rich and the poor were
equally important. The Christian religion came into existence among the
poor in an occupied nation, and spread quickly in the peasant population,
in spite of official Roman persecutions. In many ways, the conversion of
Emperor Constantine to Christianity was the "kiss of death" for the ethical
practices of a faith whose founder was a landless carpenter who brought
good news to the poor.

Judaism, Christianity, and Islam have often seen reformers try to restore
their religions' original vision of equality and the dignity of every person. The
Sufis sought to redress the caliphs' excesses by going back to the practice of
the simple life of Muhammad. The Franciscans tried to reclaim the embrace
of both ministering to the poor and the life of personal poverty practiced in
early Christianity. But, as in most cases, reformations don't succeed in changing the whole, but only create a spin-off faction that looks longingly across
the boundaries of class, wondering how things could have gone so wrong.

Both Protestantism and Catholicism have flirted with reform through modern social justice movements, though the Vatican has nearly extinguished liberation theology from its ranks, and most Protestant churches, in their silence, behave like support groups for investment bankers.

The ancient texts that I study in preparation for my classes lead me to the conclusion that if time and geography allowed, we would find Moses, Isaiah, Micah, Amos, Jesus, Muhammad, along with Martin Luther King Jr., Gandhi, Dorothy Day, and Mother Theresa sitting in the streets with the occupiers . . . While most of the rest of us just go sit on pews.

Believing in Jesus Vs Imitating Jesus

Do you believe that people will still attend public religious services in the next century? If so, will those services look much like the synagogues, churches, and mosques of today?

When you want to understand a religion that is not your own, what question do you ask first: What does your religion believe? Or, what does your religion teach you to do?

In their early years, the great religions of the world stood apart from government and the marketplace as a conscience that observed, criticized, and corrected culture. Once a religion has become incorporated into government and commerce, does the religion still exist?

The world is changing. Professions and institutions that once seemed to be permanent fixtures in the world are now passing away. It seems inevitable that the church in America will follow the churches of Europe into near extinction. Though it seems certain that some churches will thrive in America, they will be the ones that promote the mixing of consumer culture with nationalism and superstition. One is left to wonder—where we will find our moral compass?

Søren Kierkegaard warned Europeans nearly two centuries ago that the demise of the church was coming because of the church's growing irrelevance. If, he said, you propose that the faithful actually imitate Jesus, then followers will be few but profoundly influential. If, however, you suggest that being a Christian means believing in Jesus then you will have general consent of the population, and by making everyone a Christian, Christianity comes to an end. He congratulated his peers in Denmark who were beginning the stampede in exodus from institutional religion when he published that they "have constantly one guilt the less, and that a great one: you do not take part in treating God as a fool."

In a recent slip of the tongue, when I meant to say "the Council of Churches," I heard myself saying, "the Chamber of Commerce." We aging fellows often make such mistakes, but I have since wondered if it was just my weary synapses closing in on a similar sound, or if my subconscious mind has ceased to see any difference between institutional religion and the institutions of capitalism and business.

Kierkegaard believed that an ethical awareness was generally distributed in the world in the form of a conscience, but that inevitably, people will "work gradually at eclipsing their ethical and ethical-religious comprehension." We tame Christianity (or Judaism, Islam, or Buddhism for that matter) so that it serves our selfish interests, and once our conscience is subdued, religion becomes just a bit of nostalgia, good for entertainment and giving the superstitious something to do. As Kierkegaard summed it up, "Remove from the Christian religion its ability to shock, and Christianity is altogether destroyed."

In Europe, it has become obvious to the general population that solving the challenges of racism, poverty, healthcare, and environmental degradation are matters of conscience. They have made much more progress than have we Americans, who still have our big churches to assure us that such issues are not important—as long as you avoid being gay and you have Jesus in your heart. All of this can make a guy look forward to the demise of the institutional church.

And yet, as Theodore Beza reminded a provincial king in Spain four hundred years ago, "The church is an anvil on which many a hammer has been broken." Perhaps, even as the mainstream institutions of religion dissolve into the Chamber of Commerce, some anvil, some shocking, prophetic remnant of the church will survive to pester the narcissism of a new century.

Has the Church given up on Being Relevant?

When an author of pornographic novels leaves the church because the church lacks morality, should church officials pay attention?

The Archdiocese of St. Louis wanted to take millions of dollars from a Polish parish's trust fund to help pay claims in priest sex abuse cases. The congregation refused to turn over the money and was then excommunicated by its Bishop. Should the congregation have sacrificed its assets to pay victims of abuse in other congregations?

Will more churches seek to find their own moral way forward and not remain a part of larger institutions of organized religion?

Rock stars and politicians often announce dramatic religious conversions to save their careers more than to save their souls, but a decade ago, when novelist Ann Rice made headlines for becoming a Christian, she was still at the top of her popularity. This was an especially notable conversion because Rice was famous, not only for writing Vampire novels, but also for writing erotic novels under a hardly secret pseudonym.

What has not been much noted in the news is when she renounced the Christian religion, though she resolutely refused to renounce Jesus. She said, "I quit being a Christian. I'm out. In the name of Christ, I refuse to be anti-gay. I refuse to be anti-feminist. I refuse to be anti-artificial birth control. I refuse to be anti-Democrat. I refuse to be anti-secular humanism. I refuse to be anti-science. I refuse to be anti-life. In the name of Christ, I quit Christianity and being Christian."

Her post-conversion conversion is nothing new. I'm very fond of the irreverent observation attributed to comedian Lenny Bruce, who reportedly said more than fifty years ago, "Every day, people are leaving the church and going back to God."

In grad school, I realized that most of my professors at Vanderbilt Divinity School were not churchgoers. When I finally screwed up the nerve, I asked my Old Testament professor, "How am I to spend my life serving the church when my professors don't have enough faith to even attend a church?" He was not angry about my confrontation, but it was obviously a painful question. He said, "I would go if I could believe that there was a church to go to."

It took me a few more years to fully appreciate the anguish behind that answer. It is something of what Ann Rice must have felt when she said: "It's simply impossible for me to 'belong' to this quarrelsome, hostile, disputatious, and deservedly infamous group. For ten years, I've tried. I've failed. I'm an outsider. My conscience will allow nothing else."

A friend of mine, the former Roman Catholic priest, Marek Bozek, has made headlines in St. Louis and even in the *New York Times* as the archdiocese tried to get the renegade Polish congregation he serves to come back into the Catholic Church. The archbishop offered to restore the formerly excommunicated congregation, if only they would fire Bozek. The congregation of St. Stanislaus refused to do so, in part because they no longer trust the archdiocese, but also because the issue is no longer simply about respecting Polish language services. Once freed from the institutional church, the congregants also began to be inclusive of same-sex couples and to award equal roles for female members in leadership.

Once liberated from religious prejudice, it is difficult to put the genie back into the bottle. We can only hope that more people will embrace the ethics of the teachings of Jesus as the stampede continues to flee conventional religious oppression.

Are Comedians the New Princes of the Pulpit?

> Over the past decade, would you be more inclined to believe the analysis of Jon Stewart and Stephen Colbert, or the commentators on Fox or MSNBC?

> Why was there not a large and loud anti-war movement within mainstream churches during our most recent Middle Eastern wars?

> With the retirement of Jon Stewart, and Stephen Colbert's departure from the Colbert Report, where do you turn for an unvarnished take on world events?

Appearing on, "*Real Time with Bill Maher*," Cornel West, the famous Princeton professor, was challenged about his continuing religious affiliation. In spite of being sympathetic with one another's political priorities, Maher asked, "Why isn't there an anti-war movement in the church?" Of course, West has gone to jail for his participation in anti-war demonstrations, but he had to acknowledge that religious people have failed to speak up for peace in recent years.

How is it that religion in America has no generally recognized moral voice? In the middle of the last century, Bishop Fulton Sheen's sermons had more TV viewers than *I Love Lucy* or *Gunsmoke*. In those days many people could easily quote the sermons of Billy Graham, Martin Luther King Jr., and Harry Emerson Fosdick. We knew the moral writings of Dorothy Day, Reinhold and Richard Niebuhr, and Dietrich Bonhoeffer.

If you survey religious bookstores today, you will find nothing of the weight and moral force of the works of Day, Fosdick, King, or Niebuhr. While religious publications and broadcasts have multiplied, the content is generally, in a word, silly—or in two words, morally irrelevant. In the buildup to the wars in Afghanistan and Iraq, the major network news programs never challenged the obvious propaganda of the Bush administration. The church was, with only rare exception, silent (and silence is always interpreted as consent).

Who challenged the claims of the Bush administration? Most notably, it was comedians. Bill Maher's popular TV show, *Politically Incorrect*, was canceled because of his honest commentary. Jon Stewart not only ridiculed the media and the administration for their pro-war posture, but his comedy show became the most trusted news source by large demographic sections of voters during the 2004 election.

Who are the moral preachers in America today? Sadly, not one of them is associated with religion or the news media. Right up to the moment that Colbert and Steward retired, I would have said that the best moral preachers in the country are Jon Stewart, Bill Maher, and Stephen Colbert. They are all comedians, but perhaps it is the church that has become the real joke. In the 1950s and 60s, the church was the organizing heart of the Civil Rights movement. Where is that voice today?

The civil rights issue of our time has been the challenge to end the oppression of the gay community, but did the church demand an end to the "don't ask, don't tell" policy in the military? No, the public pressure came from comedians, and the movement towards reform was endorsed by generals in the armed services before we heard a word from religious leaders.

In the face of the world's most immoral disparity between the rich and the poor . . . as we continue to reel in economic malaise after more than ten years of costly and ineffective war in the Middle East . . . facing a federal budget that is cutting out nutrition programs for poor infants to maintain mortgage tax deductions on the vacation homes of the rich . . . The mainstream church is silent and in its silence has announced its own demise.

11

Philosophy and Virtue

How is it that religion in America has no generally recognized moral voice?

The Guilty and Undeserving

> Many homeless people are con men/women who tell elaborate hard luck stories to open the wallets and purses of those they meet. How far should we go to make sure our generosity is not exploited?

> Giving to panhandlers might encourage public begging and erode that person's dignity. But what is the right response to the visibly hungry and cold?

> Every city has people who are both homeless and unwelcome in local shelters. What are we to do for the unsheltered homeless?

Most people are willing, if not, in fact, eager to help those whom they regard to be either the "innocent unfortunate" or the "deserving poor." That's why, when the Catholic Church asks its members to come out in favor of putting an end to abortion, you can see responders in droves, but when they ask the members to help stop capital punishment . . . well, those meetings could typically be held in a phone booth and still leave room for Superman to make a quick change.

When a few friends and I were setting out to start a new church, we wanted to take on a project that could help to define us as a church that is concerned for the poor. We decided to build a playground for the children of the homeless who live in a local shelter. While involved in building the playground, I became aware of a much less popular subgroup among our city's poor. Next door to the homeless shelter, for whom we built the playground, was a counseling center for the unsheltered homeless. This joint effort of our local mental health agency and the homeless shelter is also a place where people who live on the street can get warm, have a cup of coffee, and sometimes a sandwich. There are also shower stalls and facilities for washing clothes.

Some of the women and men you find there may very well be innocent enough, but others are no longer welcome in any of the homeless shelters around town. Some have messed up, broken rules (or laws), or otherwise made themselves unwelcome to their family members, former employers, and even the shelters. Some have mental health issues, some have legal issues, and all of them either have or are at risk of serious health issues. Every winter, some of them die as a result of exposure, illness, or hunger. But how do we get people to care about a population that few would describe as being either deserving or innocent?

The answer, I believe, is that it has to come from the conscious decision to be the kind of people who show compassion without judgment. Understandably, not everyone wants to join that club, yet this population of street people may offer our most fundamental opportunity to serve, as Mother Theresa described them, "Jesus, in his most distressing disguise."

When winter weather rolls around, these forgotten souls are inevitably in desperate need of sleeping bags, tents, and blankets. That unused sleeping bag in your attic might save a life. The unused coat hanging in your closet, the hats and gloves you never wear, could be used by someone you may not believe really deserves your symbolic sacrifice but I believe it was St. John of the Cross who once said, "We either pass the love test or we fail entirely." Compassion, I believe, will be on the final exam.

The Philosophy of "Screw You"

Libertarians tend to love the Objectivist philosophy taught by Ayn Rand, and yet if this philosophy were broadly applied, would we still have a civilization ten years later?

Are conservative politicians and leaders in the world of finance influenced by Rand's philosophy, or are they drawn to it to justify their own greed?

Rand's disgust with her early life in a communist country inspired her insistence upon individual rights and indifference towards others. Do you think she overreacted to the abuses of communism?

In the days before computers, video games or cable TV, I wandered through my high school library in search of the thickest books on the shelf as a diversion from my rural Kentucky life where the ZIP code was "EE-I-EE-I-O." Even in my early teens, when I read the philosophical novels of Ayn Rand, it was obvious to me that her disdain for compassion and her insistence that a tacit acquiescence to the superiority of the talented and the powerful was morally childish and, if taken seriously, would result in a nightmarish world in which the strong would consume the weak.

Rand's colorful though matter-of-fact accounts of casual sex among her characters not only kept my interest, but also confirmed my suspicion that our rather conservative librarian did not actually read much or we would not have had access to *The Fountainhead*. Rand's dismissal of superstition and her disdain for the rules of elite society appealed to me as a child, in their contrast to my southern overtly religious environment, but it was clear to me that Rand's reaction to her communist-dominated early life went to a dangerous extreme.

I didn't think about Rand's "Objectivism" (also known as Ethical Egoism) again for nearly forty years, until I met some people who actually took her cruel philosophy seriously, and then, much to my surprise, I learned that Alan Greenspan, then the chairman of the Federal Reserve, was one of Rand's early disciples. That someone who had so much control over the economy actually acknowledged adherence to what amounts to economic cannibalism was a heart-stopping realization. And Greenspan is not alone among the power-elite who embrace Rand's radically self-serving views. Ron Paul is such a devoted fan that he named his now famous son, Senator Rand Paul, after her.

It should be obvious to anyone who cares about the future of our country that the growing income disparity between the vast majority of workers and the super elite will eventually allow unbridled greed to destroy our nation. Morally, indifference toward the standard of living of the masses is reprehensible, but even from an Objectivist view, if you believe that the world will still exist ten years from now, you can't push all of the world's resources into the hands of the top one percent and expect the society not to fall entirely apart. Rand insists that self-interest is the greatest good, but even those who are totally devoid of morality should be able to see past the end of their own noses. Rand's philosophy is an apologetic for greed and pleasure in the immediate moment, but it carries within it the seeds of eventual cultural collapse.

Wisconsin Congress member Paul Ryan arrived on the national stage as Mitt Romney's running mate in the 2012 presidential election. Though he is publicly a practicing Catholic, privately he has insisted that his own staff read Ayn Rand's books because, he explains, her philosophy of unchecked personal greed is, "the reason I got into public service." For years Ryan gave Rand's objectivist novel, *Atlas Shrugged*, to friends as Christmas gifts.[1]

If Rand is the philosophical guiding light to Ryan's Draconian budget proposals, we can understand why a group of outspoken nuns chartered a bus to travel around the nation, telling people that this budget is not in keeping with Catholic social teachings or basic gospel values. The choice of Ryan as the vice-presidential running mate of Mitt Romney was described as "bold." I would like to add that it might be "bold" to set your own house on fire while your family is trying to live in it, but it is still the worst possible decision you could make.

The Philosophy of Compassion

> To help the victims of a natural disaster, do you prefer to a) do nothing, b) send a donation, or c) go get involved in the clean up?

> Why does there seem to be more generosity in countries with less formal religious observance?

> In the absence of a religious mandate, we are free to choose to serve our own interests or to try to live a life of compassion. How do you choose between the two, or at least strike a defensible balance?

My first real job, when I was fifteen years old, was working on a right-of-way crew for an electric utility co-op. It was my job to fill the cooler with ice water every morning and then all day long, to drag chopped limbs and stack them into burn piles to make way for the construction of new electric lines. Our ten-hour days of manual labor, compensated at $2 an hour, were part of my inspiration to go to college.

But now, when I travel with friends to volunteer in the cleanup after Hurricane Katrina in New Orleans, to Joplin after its disastrous tornado, or

---

1. Burns, Jennifer. "Atlas Spurned."

to other disaster sites, I find myself, forty years later, piling up tree branches and carrying cases of bottle water to workers. The experience is quite different. Now I don't even make $2 an hour for the work, but the compensation is immense.

Looking around the debris field left by hurricanes and tornados, with the inevitable downed trees and twisted mounds of roofing and parts of houses and boats, I see retired people and others who have used their vacation time to come help and even unemployed people using their time productively to assist neighbors and strangers with getting back on their feet.

Americans are often generous with their time and resources to help those who are in trouble. Still, I am frequently aware that the greatest evil of our culture is not any sentiment of intentional malice, but it is indifference born of a kind of rugged individualism that has forgotten how to feel compassion toward others.

We may think that we Americans are the most generous nation on earth, but in fact, of the twenty-two most industrialized nations in the world, the United States ranks near the bottom. Per capita charitable giving in Sweden, Norway, Denmark, the Netherlands, and Luxembourg is more than four times as high as ours. Britain, France, Finland, Spain, Ireland, and Belgium are way ahead of us.[2]

Ironically, it seems that the lower a nation's average church attendance, the more likely it is that it will be generous towards the victims of disaster and poverty. That is a painful observation for me, personally, because I would love to believe that the practice of faith would increase love and compassion, rather than take the place of it. Existentially, I can testify that carrying water and stacking tree limbs to buy my first car was meaningful, but picking up disaster debris and carrying water to help a stranger is a spiritual philosophy.

Playing God

> Are you a good person if you avoid doing harm to others, or does being good require that you be a moral actor to bring about good outcomes?
>
> If you refuse to take sides in a moral dilemma, aren't you simply giving your support to the status quo?

2. Albright, *Mighty and Almighty,* 91.

If you choose to get involved in political or ethical leadership, you will not always be right. Is fear of being wrong the greatest deterrent to your willingness to take action?

Like most pastors, I'm called upon to perform many more funerals for people outside of my parish than from among our members, because those who have no church affiliation greatly outnumber those who do.

When I meet with the family members of a deceased person whom I never knew, I ask the family members what they want me to say about their loved one. Mostly, what they seem to want me to say is that their relative was a "good person." Not always, but often it seems that what they mean by "good" is what most of us mean by the word "harmless." But whenever I hear of a person being called a "good" person, I always want to know what he or she is good for.

In John Irving's wonderful novel, *Cider House Rules*, the aging Dr. Larch keeps telling one of the orphans in his care, Homer, to be useful. The setting of the novel involved ethically challenging circumstances around abortion and caring for unwanted children, but the advice of Dr. Larch reaches through the pages of fiction into our real life situations. Homer does not want to take Dr. Larch's place as the sometime physician to orphans and sometime illegal abortion doctor, because he does not want to play God. Dr. Larch points out that in fact we owe it to the world to play God, because to do nothing is, in effect, playing the part of an evil god.

Pastors often disappoint me, because they try to remain popular by always taking a neutral position on every earthly moral dilemma—which is the opposite of why we have pastors in the first place. As the Holocaust survivor, Elie Wiesel, said, "Take sides. Neutrality always serves the oppressor and never the oppressed."

I wish that evil were personified and living in a walled compound on a distant continent, so that we could simply send in an elite military squad to dispatch evil from the world. But we don't live in that universe. Evil is not in one person and not in another and much of the evil in our world hides within the complexity of our social and economic systems.

I live in a small city where more than half of our children are born into poverty. Some years there are twice as many suicides in our county as there are traffic fatalities. Unemployment is unconscionably high, and underemployment is, in my opinion, virtually criminal. Perhaps as many as 10,000 people in my community of no more than a quarter of a million people are addicted to methamphetamine, and you don't have to go very far to encounter one of the more than 800 unsheltered homeless people who live in our city.

It is not enough to be relatively harmless. We need more good people who really do want to be good for something. Plant an extra row of vegetables to share with the hungry. Be a mentor to an impoverished child. Stand up for the rights of someone you know who suffers discrimination for a disability, sexual orientation, or minority status. Sacrifice for social justice. Being neutral doesn't make you good unless your goal is to be a paperweight.

Are Bad Boys Heroes or Are They Just Bad?

> When a pro wrestler becomes a governor, or a movie star moves from the back of a horse to the White House, is it a sign of voter gullibility?
>
> Should convicted criminals from the Watergate or the Iran-Contra scandal be allowed to translate their infamy into multimillion dollar contracts in talk radio?
>
> Does the "bad boy" hero on our TV screen change the way we view real bad boys who flaunt laws and even foreign policy to accomplish their personal goals?

Hollywood has taught us to love bad boys. On the screen, cops who beat suspects to find the ticking bomb are adored, in spite of the fact that generally such beatings are a morally repugnant abuse of power. When in *The Life and Times of Judge Roy Bean*, Paul Newman portrayed the infamous Judge, he made Bean seem charming, even admirable, but that image was not accurate. The actual nineteenth century Texas judge did not just flaunt convention, he used law books as kindling to demonstrate his contempt for the law. He would hang an accused horse thief based on a decision rendered by twelve of his best customers in his saloon at the time. When presented with a case regarding a railroad boss who murdered a Chinese worker, he dismissed the case because; "there is nothing in the law about shooting a Chinaman." Bean was a monster.

The newspaper I once wrote for gave me the unsavory assignment of interviewing Oliver North (born a few miles from the Judge Roy Bean Museum in San Antonio). In 1985 it was revealed that North, in opposition to laws against selling weapons to or negotiating with terrorists, sold arms to Iran in order to gain the release of American hostages. He then gave the proceeds to the Contras in Nicaragua, against Congressional restrictions forbidding all aid to the Contras, who were, by any rational analysis, conducting a terror campaign against the poor.

North is also suspected of arranging transportation of cocaine into the United States to raise money for the Contra leaders. North illegally destroyed evidence, and in a chest-thumping display of defiance, refused to answer questions in Congressional hearings.

To be fair, a lieutenant colonel does not have the authority to do what North was found guilty of doing. Surely he took the fall for someone, and was pardoned in reward for falling on his sword. North has since earned millions of dollars in talk radio and on the speaking circuit, playing the role of a hero, in spite of being guilty of mass murder and treason.

In 2006 he returned to Nicaragua to campaign against the reelection of President Daniel Ortega. Though he had no political or military status, he knew that his presence would be interpreted as a threat of a return of American-backed terrorism. Of course, being very tired of American interference in their country, they did reelect Ortega.

America desperately needs heroes but, as Confucius said, "One does not plaster a dung wall." North is not a hero.

12

Personal Musings

"News is what somebody does not want you to print. All the rest is advertising."

Organized Labor and Higher Education

Has the concept of tenure lived beyond its useful time in higher education? A tenured professor often feels trapped in a "golden cage," preventing a more natural movement around the nation's various colleges and universities. Would students be better served if there were more movement among faculty?

Tenure is granted in most universities in a process that relies heavily on peer review. Do you believe that your current employment would be secure if the people in your office got to vote on your tenure?

The concept of adjunct professors was to allow professionals to occasionally teach a class in their area of expertise, but because tenured positions have become less common, many academics have found themselves working permanently as a very low-paid adjunct, teaching several classes for more than one college and still living in poverty. Should adjuncts be allowed to unionize and demand more fair treatment from the institutions they serve?

While many nations have elected to invest in their own future by making higher education either free or easily affordable, in the United States, the cost of earning a college degree is becoming increasingly prohibitive. Still, though the costs to students seem to be a huge hurdle, there is also a cost to being employed in higher education. In many smaller cities, the local university is the largest employer in town, yet most of the jobs are at the bottom of the wage scale. In the case of adjunct professors who are symbolically compensated per class, being an indentured servant might start to look like a good deal.

One of the things that has inspired me to continue to contend with the nasty and irrational politics of parish ministry is the fact that my other real option would be to teach, and if there is anything that makes the shamefully dishonest politics of religious institutions seem benign, it is the politics of a college campus. As former Secretary of State Henry Kissinger is famous for saying, "The politics on a college campus are so fierce because the stakes are so small." And sure enough, some of the departmental fights can make a faculty meeting look like it is actually Darwin's waiting room.

Professors who are lucky enough to escape the adjunct track face a fairly unique employment issue that most of us never get or have to fret over: tenure. Our universities attempt to recruit the best among scholars to move to a community and more or less permanently spend their lives educating locals. However, it is difficult to tell when you have actually been hired. Being given a "tenure track" position means that you will remain under scrutiny by your peers for several years. You must literally apply for the position you hold over and over and over again, publishing, volunteering, and forswearing both family and personal life in the hope of eventually being granted tenure.

If, God forbid, you fail to be awarded tenure, then it is exceedingly unlikely that any other college will ever offer you another chance. You have already been judged to be unfit. You may spend ten or twelve years of your life and rack up debt in the six figures in order to apply for that position. If you are not awarded tenure, your degrees may be virtually worthless, though you are expected to continue to pay for them. Clearly, tenure is intended to protect professors from being dismissed for inappropriate motivations so that universities may foster freedom of thought and creativity. However, if the process becomes tainted with personality conflicts or petty rivalries (or romances), then an excellent teacher, outstanding scholar, and valuable citizen can be kicked to the curb for no sane reason.

If this were only a hypothetical issue it would hardly be worth your time to consider. However, it is not a hypothetical. Excellent professors who also happen to be parents and spouses have their lives and careers ruined through treacherous, gossip-laden peer review. Kissinger said that the stakes were small, but they are not small if you are on the receiving end of a power-abusing gladiatorial contest. If the goal is to avoid unionized faculty, administrators must work diligently to remove abuse from the employment system.

Saying What Needs to Be Said When No One Wants to Listen

> While there may be no such thing as objective news reporting, what source do you rely upon the most to give you accurate information with the least amount of commentary?
>
> If you attend religious services, do you believe that your priest/rabbi/pastor/imam is free to speak the truths that she or he holds dear, or does she or he have to carefully adjust her or his message to suit the audience and associated judicatory authorities?
>
> Do journalists have a professional obligation to educate the public, even regarding those inconvenient truths about which they might prefer to not know?

I may be the only person in history ever escorted out of a Kiwanis meeting for my own protection. My Fourth of July address was intended to provoke thought, but I must have overshot my goal, and instead provoked a fistfight. It seemed reasonable to me, on a day when we were celebrating our liberation from tyrannical colonialism, we might think about how we in the United States were militarily enforcing our economic colonialism in Central America and Africa. It was clear that several people did not appreciate my efforts at reality orientation, but one red-faced pastor had to be held back from pulling me off the stage by his fellow social club members while I safely escaped through the kitchen and into the parking lot.

Though the content of my speech was broadly deemed to have been as inappropriate for the Fourth of July as was Rosanne Barr's 1990 off-key rendition of the National Anthem at a Padres baseball game, the club members still insisted that my ordained attacker send me an apology. They should have also proofread his letter, because it was largely an apologetic for why he should have beaten me senseless.

I was just a young graduate student at the time and the angry minister was already retired, so he concluded his letter with an attempt at giving me career advice. He said that he knew what audiences liked to hear, and by saying only what they liked, he had enjoyed a very successful career.

His sage advice to me was: Carefully study your audience and practice saying just what they wanted to hear. I should have framed that piece of correspondence, because it stands out in my memory as an unintended archetype for many future conversations with church officials.

In my generation-long tenure as an opinion writer for the *Springfield News-Leader*, I tried to bear in mind the maxim that "news is what somebody does not want you to print. All the rest is advertising."[1] This sentiment is also found in the pseudo-Pauline New Testament letter, 2 Timothy, warning the young preacher against those who insist upon having their ears tickled by being told only what they want to hear (2 Timothy 4:3). That does not mean that either opinion writing or preaching should be intentionally insulting, but it does mean that both should have an unflinching devotion to saying what needs to be said, in the interests of having an informed, critical-thinking public.

Viewers of Fox News are astonishingly unconcerned about research that indicates that most of what they hear on Fox is simply not true. MSNBC viewers seem to be willing to accept that they are being fed a constant stream of political analysis with very little substantive news dropped in between segments of partisan vitriol. And CNN seems now to be devoted to becoming the *People* magazine of mindless entertainment masquerading as news.

Consider the time and energy given to President Clinton's office affair. How newsworthy was the incident, and how much time did it get in the broadcast media? Sadly, because of the nature of our news sources, you already know the names of consenting adults involved, what color dress she was wearing, and which tobacco product he was holding in his hand. However, this same media has failed to tell us how many civilians have been killed in President Obama's deployment of predator drones, or how many civilians were killed in our invasions of Iraq and Afghanistan. There has been no media discussion as to why no one has gone on trial for treason or war crimes after it became clear that the reasons given for going to war were falsified, and that prisoners of war were tortured. But please, do go on with your discussion of the possible deportation of Justin Bieber . . . really, I'm dying to know more . . . because the media-consuming public has apparently forgotten how to blush.

1. Quote Investigator

Being Famous Vs Being Important

> Personally, I don't ever publicly use the names of mass murderers
> because I do not think those people deserve to become "famous"
> for having committed heinous acts. Do you think that the news
> media should also refrain from making people famous for all the
> wrong reasons?

> Most of us could quickly name three or four politicians or movie
> stars who have a history of being arrested for drunk driving. Pub-
> lic shamming hardly seems like an appropriate response to a sub-
> stance abuse problem but if a friend of yours confessed to having
> a drinking problem, would you know when and where there is a
> nearby AA meeting she or he might attend?

> We know the names and recognize the faces of the "talking heads"
> in the media, but does that familiarity in any way mean that those
> persons are either knowledgeable or important?

The late Erma Bombeck once said, "Never confuse fame and success.
Madonna is one. Mother Teresa is the other." It is not only possible to be
famous without being important, but in our media-driven age, it is likely.
The distinction between being famous and being important was blurred by
my home state by the induction of Rush Limbaugh into the Hall of Famous
Missourians, placing the talk show hate-monger into the same short list
that includes such important names as Samuel Clemens (the Hall's first in-
ductee) and Dred Scott (eighteenth-century abolitionist who was inducted
just days before Limbaugh).

The bust of Limbaugh was placed in the Capitol rotunda in a secret
ceremony under armed guard because of recent vociferous protests against
placing his likeness among such figures as Harry Truman, George Washington Carver, Edwin Hubble, Walter Cronkite, Walt Disney, and Reinhold
Niebuhr. Limbaugh, however, seemed to believe that he belonged there, and
said of those of us who have objected, "They're deranged. They're literally
deranged." I wish that the bust of Sacajawea could speak to tell Limbaugh
what she would think of his misogynist rants against a female law school
student whom he called a "slut" and a "prostitute." I suspect that "deranged"
would be a mild epithet compared to what she would likely call him.

Limbaugh's quarter century of broadcasts have made him unavoidably
well-known, though I'm not sure that's what we really mean by "famous."
When confronted with his racist, misogynist, gay bashing, anti-immigrant,

hate- mongering statements, he often waves them off as "entertainment," insisting that he cannot be held responsible for his hate filled rants. But when he is not in trouble, he is in the warm embrace of the Republican Party, with many feeling that he represents a fearless articulation of true Republican values.

Pastorally, I have often objected to Rush and the whole industry of turning angry, racist, woman hating, gay bashing, immigrant scapegoating rhetoric into entertainment. There are things in life about which we should be angry, but as Aristotle said, "Anyone can become angry—that is easy. But to be angry with the right person, to the right degree, at the right time, for the right purpose, and in the right way—that is not easy."

The too easy anger of talk radio can make a person of genuinely evil intent feel self-righteous. Anger can make an entirely uninformed individual feel smug and superior. Anger can make society's victims believe that the very people who oppress them are their saviors, and their fellow victims are to blame for their misery. Anger does not make a person smart or well informed or patriotic. In this case, it just turns the gullible into dangerous voters.

Voting with Your Feet (And a Broomstick)

Have you ever attended a protest or rally when you knew that your cause had no chance of success but you felt the need to stand up and be counted, even in the face of certain failure?

Political movements have employed deceptive propaganda to garner support from people who have resisted a more fact-based approach to educating the public. Our national founders were not above using such tactics to start the American Revolution. In such a case, do the ends justify the means?

Has the advent of online polls and emailed petitions made it too easy to express yourself from your home without ever actually voting with your feet by attending a political event?

During my most recent sabbatical, I had the opportunity to live in the Boston area for a few months. I've not been a great student of American Revolutionary history, but the proximity to the Freedom Trail, the Minute Man Trail, and the North Church of Paul Revere fame, along with Bunker Hill and Faneuil Hall made the topic impossible to ignore. What I found most fascinating about the birth of the revolution that brought about our democracy was how much work had to go into persuading farmers, blacksmiths, bakers, and candlestick makers to leave hearth and home to attend meetings to discuss the ideas of the revolution and the plans for making their dreams come true. They used sermons and newspaper articles, but they also used jingles and outrageous propaganda so that people who couldn't be persuaded into participation could at least be tricked into showing up when needed!

Each day, when I had finished my historical inquiries and returned to my suburban apartment to read my email, I was offered multiple opportunities to click on an internet site to sign a petition protesting the war, advocating for alternative energy, opposing anti-gay constitutional amendments, or otherwise standing tall and being counted in the cause of truth, liberty, and justice – all from the little desk in my study. Would Ben Franklin have circulated an Internet petition expressing his disdain for British rule, and if he had, would anyone have left his or her computer screens to show up at Bunker Hill?

The information superhighway makes unfiltered information much more available, but it also gives us the false sense that we have done something when we sign our names to a form letter. Aids in congressional offices will tell you that such correspondence has little or no impact on congressional votes.

Many times in the past few years I've responded to an invitation to a rally or protest sent out to thousands of subscribers to ProVote, MoveOn. org, Concerned Scientists, One.org, and Faithful America, only to find that of five or six thousand recipients, five or six of us show up. A hundred people showing up at a senator's office protesting his or her connection to big oil and big pharma will get a senator's attention. Five people showing up just looks pathetic.

It may be apocryphal, but I have heard of an incident during the Civil War when the armies of the North and the South were sweeping through rural Missouri on their way to a conflict, when an elderly woman came racing out of a cabin holding her broom over her head to join the fray. A young soldier beside her said, "You better go home, Grandma, you can't do much with that broom." And she replied, "At least I can show them whose side I'm on!"

Our generation has some passionate opinions about a lot of difficult issues, but just having an opinion doesn't mean much if you are not willing to lift your broom over your head and join the fray.

Promising Pie in the Sky

> We have the quality of government that we elect, so what might be the best way to educate voters on the issues and improve the public's critical thinking skills?

> No one can reasonably blame politicians for trying to win votes by saying what voters want to hear, but shouldn't our campaign process have some kind of "Snopes" tool that lets us know when political speech equates to "pants on fire"?

> Campaign rhetoric has promised militarily aggressive foreign policy, longer prison sentences for domestic criminals, and a great deal of legislation to govern personal moral decisions. When enacted as policy, have any of these things attained the desired objectives?

When I was a lad, a candidate for our Kentucky state legislature campaigned on the promise to "bring our boys home from Vietnam," in spite of the fact that state legislators had no say in the matter. Similarly, has anyone ever been legislated into being straight? Obviously, if someone is straight because it is illegal to be gay, then that person is, in fact, still gay. So, politicians, please, just mind your own business.

I understand that some people have religious convictions about abortion, but this is not a nation governed by any one religion. So please, keep your beliefs out of legislation and allow individuals to manage their own bodies based on their own beliefs.

We elect a government to create a healthy environment for commerce and to manage national defense. A reasonable argument can be articulated that the government is failing in an abysmal way to do those two things we "hired" them to do. There are a few things that are sinking state and federal budgets under lethal debt, and they need to be addressed honestly and quickly:

1. You cannot point to any democracy created at the end of a gun. The very idea is embarrassingly stupid. The wars in Afghanistan and Iraq gave birth to new generations of potential future terrorists, and were never successful in decreasing the threat of terrorism. The resources spent on these clearly unnecessary wars hurt us both financially and morally. All such military adventurism must be avoided in the future.

2. We have about 2.3 million people in jails and prisons at an average cost to tax payers of $22,000 each per year. Most of these prisoners do not represent a danger to society. They are in prison to fatten the construction and supply contracts of politically connected businesses profiting from the penal system. We could immediately release non-violent criminals and save $20 billion.

3. Stop merely talking about alternative energy and environmental issues, and do something productive. We have enough wind energy in Montana and solar energy in Arizona to power the nation. What we don't have is an energy grid to move the electricity to where it is needed. So build the grid already, and stop protecting oil and coal profits!

4. Stop lying about healthcare, kick the insurance companies out of the equation, and come up with a real plan. Western European countries and Canada have healthcare that is demonstrably superior to ours, covering everyone and spending half as much money as we do. Your jokes about Canadian healthcare are just smoke and mirrors so you can keep shoveling money to pharmaceutical and insurance companies. We're onto you, so knock it off.

The Republicans gave us a prescription meds bill that was written by the pharmaceutical companies for their own profits, and the Democrats have given us a healthcare reform bill that created 30,000,000 more premium-paying customers and does little to address runaway costs.

As Bob Marley so eloquently sang, free yourselves from intellectual slavery, because none but ourselves can free our minds. We must stop electing people who fill the air with jargon but do not address the real issues.

It's Good to Be the King

If you could have a one-year term as an absolute monarch in the United States, what would you try to accomplish?

Clearly, lobbyists' political donations prevent many meaningful transformations in the United States. How can we effectively get money out of politics?

Can capitalism be combined with socialism to move toward full employment while protecting our environment?

In Mel Brooks' comedy, *"History of the World, Part 1"* Brooks plays the part of the wanton French king, Louis XVI. Frequently, while enjoying the carnal pleasures of his position, he looks at the camera and says, "It's good to be the king." In these days of political gridlock when nothing seems to be getting done, I'm tempted to fantasize about what an enlightened despot might do in this country.

If I could be the king, I would end all military involvement in foreign nations and embark on a worldwide effort to provide clean water and basic education to the world. We could accomplish this for about twenty percent of what we spent on the wars in Iraq and Afghanistan. Clean water and education would do more to end international terrorism than any of our military efforts have done so far.

I would take the remainder of the saving from this military adventurism and invest it in clean energy mass transit projects. The largest single deterrent to moving from welfare to work is reliable transportation. The largest single challenge to our environment and to public safety is our addiction to the automobile. We need to start changing that at a rapid pace.

I would also begin an immediate project of modernizing the nation's electricity grid. While the burning of coal continues to be necessary to satisfy the nation's need for energy, the coal should be burned on the site where it is mined, and the electricity moved to where it is needed. It is a waste of resources to move the coal all over the nation to burn where there is electricity demand. The grid would also make it possible to move electricity from solar and wind farms and ocean wave generation points to the places of highest population concentration. In a very few years, there would be no more need to burn coal and natural gas. To maintain employment, I would create solar panel and wind turbine assembly plants in communities where there are coal mines now, so that miners could easily transition from a dirty energy job into a clean energy job.

How would I pay for the new grid? Easy: prison reform. Thirty years ago we had 24,000 federal prisoners. Now we have 209,000, with negligible impact on the crime rate, though it has certainly become a huge federal expense. Violent criminals should be imprisoned to protect society; all others should serve their time in home incarceration and be made to work to repay the victims of their crimes while paying taxes on their incomes. All prisons should become self-supporting through light manufacturing that is also geared toward teaching skills for employment after incarceration. Prison shouldn't be about societal revenge. It is to protect us from violent criminals, and to reform human beings so that they can be employed taxpayers.

If I were king, university education would be free. An educated population earns more money and pays more in taxes. This is not a giveaway; this is revenue producing. Look at the countries where education is free now and note how their economy is doing relative to ours.

It is not very likely that I will ever be appointed King of America, but if we got money out of politics, wouldn't we immediately have a government that would set about attempting to accomplish these goals democratically?

An Abrupt Ending

On my first long bike ride of the season, a friend and member of my church cabinet asked me why I still write a column for the *Springfield News-Leader*. He said, "You must be a masochist to keep taking all of the hate mail." At our next rest stop, I checked my email on my phone and showed him two letters from readers that had just come in thanking me for my last column. "I write for these people," I explained. The hate mail, an occasional stalker, and threats left on the telephone answering machine are the price you pay to keep progressive ideas in the public conversation.

By the time we were loading our bikes at the end of our day's ride, another email arrived, inviting me to a meeting where I would be told of changes on the Opinion Page where my column appeared. Of course, the only reason to tell me would be if I were the change. I had a jumble of emotions upon receiving this news that I would soon be a "former" columnist.

I had a regular column for nearly a decade, and had been a contributing writer for more than twenty years. There is only one citywide paper where I live, and it seems that most local writers have had no more than a year or two on the page, so I am deeply grateful to have had this opportunity for such a long time. And I can certainly understand that it is reasonable to pass this coveted space on to another writer.

Still, I realize that most of the people I personally know now are connections originally made in response to my columns. When I have thought of giving it up in the past, I was always stopped by the awareness of how many friendships started in the correspondence that comes each time my liberal musings were published.

Every time someone walks up to me in a restaurant and asks, "Are you Roger Ray?" I study the questioner's face before I answer, trying to discern whether this reader has a favorable impression of my work, or if I am about to hear an unsolicited criticism. As poet and musician Bruce Cockburn has written, we live our lives like an axe falling through water, leaving no trace. I'm okay with that. I realize that I will soon be left to finish my meals in anonymous peace and someone else will be experiencing the blessings and curses of being a liberal writer in a very conservative community. I want to thank all of my faithful readers . . . the ones who liked my columns and the ones who didn't, but especially for all of you who have said to me, "You made me think."

I endured the criticisms and appreciated the praise, but most of all, I wrote for those who were willing to reconsider the important topics I have tried to keep in public conversation. Keep thinking, and keep working for social justice. Peace be with you.

Bibliography

ACLU, "Race and the Death Penalty." Online: https://www.aclu.org/race-and-death-penalty?redirect=capital-punishment/race-and-death-penalty.

Albright, Madeline. *The Mighty and the Almighty: Reflections on America, God, and World Affairs.* New York: Harper-Collins 2006.

Badash, David. "Chick-Fil-A 5 Reasons It Isn't What You Think It Is." *Huffington Post*, August 1, 2012. Online: http://www.huffingtonpost.com/david-badash/chick-fil-a-5-reasons-it-isnt-what-you-think_b_1725237.html

Before It's News, "IL State Representative Compares Chicago Gun Laws to Castration." February 27, 2013. Online: http://beforeitsnews.com/alternative/2013/02/il-state-representative-compares-chicago-gun-laws-to-castration-video-2578552.html

Bihari, Michael. "Why Are Medications Cheaper to Buy in Canada?" *About Health*, September 26, 2013. Online: http://drugs.about.com/od/faqsaboutyourdrugs/f/Canada_cheap.htm

Bradford, Harry. "These 10 Companies Control Enormous Number of Consumer Brands," *Huffington Post*, April 27, 2012. Online: http://www.huffingtonpost.com/2012/04/27/consumer-brands-owned-ten-companies-graphic_n_1458812.html

Brown, Peter. "GMO Myths and Truths," *Earth Open Source*, November 9, 2014. Online: http://earthopensource.org/?s=gmo+myths+and+truths

Burns, Jennifer. "Atlas Spurned." *New York Times*, August 14, 2012. Online: http://www.nytimes.com/2012/08/15/opinion/ayn-rand-wouldnt-approve-of-paul-ryan.html

Cascio, Wayne. "The High Cost of Low Wages," *Harvard Business Review*, December 2006. Online: https://hbr.org/2006/12/the-high-cost-of-low-wages/ar/1

Center for American Progress. "Green Recovery." Online: http://www.peri.umass.edu/fileadmin/pdf/other_publication_types/peri_report.pdf

Day, Dorothy, Wikiquote. Online: https://en.wikiquote.org/wiki/Dorothy

Death Penalty Information, "Facts about Deterrence and the Death Penalty." Online: http://www.deathpenaltyinfo.org/facts-about-deterrence-and-death-penalty

Death Penalty Information Center, "Innocence List." Online: http://www.deathpenaltyinfo.org/innocence-list-those-freed-death-row

Levinson, Jessica. "Supreme Court ruling: As if we don't have enough money in politics already." *L A Times*, April 3, 2014. Online: http://www.latimes.com/opinion/commentary/la-oe-levinson-campaign-finance-mccutcheon-20140403,0,404480.story#axzz2yLv7vY9E

Huffington Post. "Obama Muslim Rumors Persist Among Illinois Republicans: 39 Percent Believe President Is Muslim," March 20, 2012. Online: http://www.huffingtonpost.com/2012/03/20/nearly-half-of-illinois-g_n_1367759.html

Huffington Post. "The U.S. Illiteracy Rate Hasn't Changed In 10 Years," September 6, 2013. Online: http://www.huffingtonpost.com/2013/09/06/illiteracy-rate_n_3880355.html

Krugman, Paul. "Fiscal Fever Breaks," *New York* Times, December 30, 2012. Online: http://www.nytimes.com/2013/12/30/opinion/krugman-fiscal-fever-breaks.html?_r=0

Mallick, Heather. "Ontario's new anti-bullying 'gay-straight' law was born of heroism," *The Star*, June 1, 2012. Online: http://www.thestar.com/opinion/editorialopinion/article/1206501—ontario-s-new-anti-bullying-gay-straight-law-was-born-of-heroism?bn=1

Maheshwari, Sapna and Sanders, Rachel. "Big Food Is Quietly Spending Millions To Prevent GMO Labeling In The U.S." *Buzz Feed*, October 29, 2013. Online: http://www.buzzfeed.com/rachelysanders/big-food-spending-millions-to-prevent-gmo-labeling#.siqgD8VAZ

Mercola, Joseph. "The 9 Foods the U.S. Government is Paying You to Eat,"*Mercola.com*, August 3, 2011. Online: http://articles.mercola.com/sites/articles/archive/2011/08/03/the-9-foods-the-us-government-is-paying-you-to-eat.aspx

NPR. "Who Are The Undecided Voters?" October 31, 2008. Online: http://www.npr.org/templates/story/story.php?storyId=96403104

Nurse, Paul. "Stamp Out Anti-Science in US Politics." *New Scientists*, September 14, 2011. Online: http://www.newscientist.com/article/mg21128302.900

Pollen, Robert and Garrett-Peltier, Heidi. "The U.S. Employment Effects of Military and Domestic Spending Priorities: An Updated Analysis." Online: http://www.peri.umass.edu/fileadmin/pdf/published_study/spending_priorities_PERI.pdf

Quote Investigator, Online: http://quoteinvestigator.com/2013/01/20/news-suppress/

Reich, Robert. "Why Inequality is the Real Cause of Our Ongoing Terrible Economy," Online: http://robertreich.org/post/9789891366

Southey, Tabitha. "Archbishop Chooses the Wrong Cause to Play the Martyr." *The Globe and Mail*, June 2, 2012. Online: http://www.theglobeandmail.com/commentary/ontario-archbishop-chooses-the-wrong-cause-to-play-the-martyr/article4226019/

Tailor, Monalisa and Stillman, Michael. "Dead Man Walking. *New England Journal of Medicine*, November 14, 2013. Online: http://www.nejm.org/doi/full/10.1056/NEJMp1312793

Taranto, James. "Heritage Rewrites History." *Wall Street Journal*, February 8, 2012. Online: http://online.wsj.com/news/articles/SB10001424052970204369404577211161144786448

Wikipedia, "List of Countries by Infant Mortality Rate." Online: http://en.wikipedia.org/wiki/List_of_countries_by_infant_mortality_rate

Wikipedia, "The Masque of Anarchy." Online: https://en.wikipedia.org/wiki/The_Masque_of_Anarchy

Wikipedia, "World Health Organization Ranking of Health Systems." Online: http://en.wikipedia.org/wiki/World_Health_Organization_ranking_of_health_systems